The Seven Bridges: A Handbook for a Christ-Centered Marriage

ISBN 978-1-329-61999-9

Table of Contents

Appendix: Couch Time! Questions

Introduction

There are many great books about marriage in print today. You can find a book on just about any topic or issue as it pertains to marriage. We have read many of them and find the information invaluable. They have forged new paths into understanding relationships and marriage.

So, why would we feel the need to add one more resource to the world's library on marriage? One thing we have learned through the years in talking with couples, researching relationships and working on our own marriage is that relationships are incredibly complicated, although they tend to respond in very predictable ways. Many of the couples we have worked with over the years have also read and developed a great appreciation for the works of many of the great marriage authors. Yet, they still find themselves facing many challenges in their relationships. This led us to further explore whether there were additional insights we could gain into relationships. What really makes them healthy? Not just able to survive, but healthy, growing and thriving.

One day it struck us. God designed marriage, so why not look at what he designed? After all, would he not create something that was perfect? Not only is he the author and perfecter of our faith (Hebrews 12:2), but he is also the author and perfecter of marriage. We decided to start from the beginning, the very beginning. We took a clean sheet of paper, cleared our minds and decided to look to scripture starting in Genesis to see if we could unravel this great design. We knew that God brought Adam and Eve together in marriage in the second chapter of Genesis, but we still had questions. How did God intend marriage to work on a day to day basis? What would he say makes a successful marriage? After all, one would think that the creator of the universe didn't design marriage just to survive. He is the great creator! Wouldn't he expect it to grow and accomplish something? As we began to read through scripture with this in mind, the information was astonishing. Just like sorting through pieces of a puzzle, a picture began to emerge that was inspiring. This was it! This is what God designed, and it made all the sense in the world.

As you read through this book, we ask that you also start from the beginning. Let go of your prior expectations about marriage and relationships. Take one step at a time and begin to let God shape a new understanding for you. We hope you are challenged and find new insights not only in your view of marriage, but also in your relationship with God.

We have been married for 18 years and we jokingly say "it's been the best 17 years of our life together." It is by God's grace that we have made it and by His grace we will continue to make it. We are two imperfect people relying on God for our marriage.

Throughout our marriage we struggled with each of the issues we will be walking through in this book. We call them bridges. We have also had the privilege of walking other couples through these bridges. When you think about a bridge, what comes to your mind? A bridge is an over pass that takes you from one destination to another over impassable terrains. If you have ever been to Spaghetti Junction in Atlanta, you will have seen bridge upon bridge with lots of confusion. If you do not focus on the bridge that you need to be on, you could either cause a wreck or miss your exit resulting in the need to travel back across one of those bridges to get you back on the right road. That is how the bridges in this book work. You need to travel over each bridge one at a time. You will also likely need to revisit each bridge at different points in your marriage. This is not backtracking. This is like taking a new vacation. The destination may be different but the route to get there might have some similarities to a prior trip and you may need to cross a familiar bridge. Some journey's may take longer, but do not give up. The destination is worth it!

One of the biggest problems we have seen in many of the couples that we have worked with is the issue of expectations. Expectations of what their spouse should or should not do. Just because your mother or father did it one way, does not mean your spouse will do it the same way. In our workshops, we ask each spouse to write out their expectations. Once they write them down, we then ask them to tear them up. We encourage each couple to let go of as many expectations as possible. The changes you try to make happen in your spouse will often be doomed to failure and will only bring disappointment to both of you. Instead ask the Lord to make the needed changes in you! Your spouse will follow. Your greatest expectation must be from God, not your spouse. Psalm 62:5 states "My soul waits silently for God alone, for my expectation is from Him."

As you read this book, understand that it is not intended to be a light read. It is designed to make you think, ponder, reflect, and likely change. Not every topic is explored in fine detail. We want you to explore the detail in a personalized way that is tailored for your marriage. We have included relevant scripture passages that we encourage you to spend time praying over and considering what the Lord might want to communicate to you. What does God want to do in your relationship with him and in your marriage?

Good luck.

Chapter 1: The Great Design

As we begin the process of understanding how God designed marriage, we need to consider a concept that exists with any design whether it is an airplane, bridge, highway or building. All designs have parts that hold it together and these parts operate together based on a foundational principle.   For example, the wings of an airplane are a necessary part of the design.   However, the wings by themselves do not make the airplane fly. It takes the principle of aerodynamics applied to the wings of the airplane as it thrusts forward, along with all the other parts, to make it work as designed. All the parts have to work together in the right way based on a foundational principle. A wing on its own would fall like a stone when dropped off a cliff. However, when it is put in the right place and works with all the other plane parts, it lifts the plane allowing it to fly. Marriage is not dissimilar. It has many parts to make it work, but those parts must work together and operate around a foundational principle for it to function as God designed. This is where many couples struggle as they try to overcome certain issues in their marriage. They spend all their time focusing on fixing the broken parts in their marriage, and then apply those fixed parts to a flawed foundational principle that exists in their relationship.

For example, one of the most common issues many couples face is poor communication. Consider the following couple, Mike and Stephanie. They were upset because every conversation they had seemed to end in a fight. Each one would say that they never intended their conversations to end up that way, but no matter how friendly the conversation started, it always ended in frustration. They just couldn't seem to communicate with each other. They went to counseling and learned some great ways to communicate more effectively. At first, they noticed a remarkable improvement. However, over the course of the next few months, their conversations began to fall back into the same habits. They became even more frustrated because they knew "how" to communicate, but they just couldn't seem to make it happen. They, like many couples, found themselves at a decision point. We can either divorce or accept that we are not good communicators and live in a strained marriage.

Mike and Stephanie recognized that they had a broken part in their marriage. They even found a way to trade that part (poor communication) in for a more advanced part for healthy communication. They thought that it would make their marriage that much stronger. The problem is that they found themselves implementing a new part without properly applying it to the design. Their marriage was not operating on the foundational principle of God's design for marriage. In other words, they were a state of the art airplane that sat in the hangar.

We want couples to learn to take their marriage out of the hangar and fly to new heights. We all have parts in our marriage that are in need of repair or replacement. However, we must learn to apply those new parts within the foundational principle of the marriage design. So what is this foundational principle? Let's begin by exploring God's view of marriage in scripture.

"I hate divorce, says the Lord God of Israel"

-   Malachi 2:16

"Haven't you read," he replied, "that at the beginning the Creator 'made them male and female,' and said, 'For this reason a man will leave his father and mother and be united to his wife, and the two will become one flesh'? So they are no longer two, but one. Therefore what God has joined together, let man not separate."

-   Matthew 19:4-6

Jesus replied, "Moses permitted you to divorce your wives because your hearts were hard. But it was not this way from the beginning. I tell you that anyone who

divorces his wife, except for marital unfaithfulness, and marries another woman
commits adultery."

-   Matthew 19:8-9

It is very clear in scripture that God wants married couples to remain together throughout their life on earth. He views marriage as a covenant bond that he binds together. While our wedding vows express our commitment to our spouse, it is important to recognize that God views himself as the one that binds the couple together and establishes the covenant. Our wedding vows represent our acceptance of the covenant that God has established. Knowing that God wants marriage to last is probably not new information to most people. However, it does raise another question. Why does God believe it is necessary for the marriage relationship to be a covenant? Why not just a mutual agreement, contract or general understanding? Let's explore God's view of marriage in scripture in more detail.

For your Creator will be your husband; the Lord of Heaven's Armies in his name!
He is your Redeemer, the Holy One of Israel, the God of all the earth.

- Isaiah 54:5

Your children will commit themselves to you, O Jerusalem, just as a young man
commits himself to his bride. Then God will rejoice over you as a bridegroom
rejoices over his bride.

-   Isaiah 62:5

"The time is coming," declares the Lord, "when I will make a new covenant with
the house of Israel and with the house of Judah. It will not be like the covenant I
made with their forefathers when I took them by the hand to lead them out of
Egypt, because they broke my covenant, though I was a husband to them,"
declares the Lord.

- Jeremiah 31:31-32

This is where the marriage design begins to unfold and reveal itself. God views his relationship to mankind as a marriage! He says that he is our husband and that he rejoices over us just like a bridegroom over his bride. He views his commitment to us in the same context as a marriage commitment. Both are a covenant. God wants our marriage to be a covenant, because marriage is supposed to be a reflection of the covenant relationship of God to mankind. In order for us to truly understand God's design for marriage, we must appreciate the importance of this concept.

Marriage was never designed by God to be temporary. It is a serious commitment that requires serious intention. It should not be taken lightly or considered on a whim. Having said that, we know of marriages that started on a whim, but the couples later recognized the importance of the commitment and became serious in their intentions and focus on developing and growing in their marriage relationship. A marriage will never develop into a healthy and growing relationship if it is not taken serious. This is not unlike our relationship with Christ. The maturity of our Christian faith is a direct result of how serious and intentional we are about our relationship with Christ.

When one desires to strengthen their faith, they typically spend more time in prayer, reading God's word, regularly attending church, fellowship with other Christians, reading Christian books and other resources. In other words, they do everything they can to expose themselves to things that will help them become more mature in their faith. However, knowledge is not enough. We need to learn to live out our faith. There are certain foundational attributes that reflect a growing and healthy relationship with God.

As we have worked with struggling couples over the years, we noticed recurring themes that emerged in these marriages regardless of the particular struggle they were facing. These themes reflected common attributes that were missing or broken down in the relationship. We also noticed that these same themes were present and active in couples that were growing and thriving in their marriage. What is even more interesting is that we found these same attributes had a similar impact on a person's relationship with God. Once we began to reflect on the fact that God views his relationship to mankind as a marriage, it all started to make sense. This is part of the great design. The same attributes that are present in a growing and healthy relationship with God are also the same attributes that should be present in a growing and healthy marriage. After all, our relationship to God is a marriage. These attributes are the parts that must all work together based upon a common foundational principle in order for a marriage to work as designed. If the foundational principle is that marriage is a reflection of God's relationship to mankind, then the parts of that relationship are humility, forgiveness, healing, patience, fellowship, purpose and celebration.

Think about it this way. God desires to heal each one of us and bring us into fellowship with him. However, before we can be healed, we must first humble ourselves and seek his forgiveness. Christ himself demonstrated great humility by taking the very nature of a servant, and is eager to forgive all who are willing. Of course, the healing process often takes time and requires much patience. Once we are restored into a right relationship with God, he desires to engage us into his purpose in order to accomplish the works of his kingdom, and to celebrate that our names a written in heaven.

Now, just knowing the individual parts is not enough. You have to know how each part is designed and the keys to making them work. Otherwise, we get caught in the trap of just using "buzz-words" but don't ever get them truly implemented into our lives. We need to take the time to explore each of these attributes and understand them from God's perspective and how they are portrayed in scripture. It is with this understanding that we are able to really grow and break old habits and patterns that constrain us.

The next seven chapters will explore each one of the attributes. We will explore each on the following seven dimensions:

1. What is the attribute
2. Why the attribute is important
3. The things that hinder the attribute
4. The things that promote the attribute
5. How the attribute is demonstrated by God
6. How the attribute is demonstrated in marriage
7. Steps to implementing the attribute

As we discuss each of these attributes, it is important to appreciate that marriage is a journey; a great journey. It is a life long journey traveled with your closest companion. It has many challenges, but the journey also presents a unique opportunity for adventure and great reward for those willing to go on that journey. Successful journeys require an understanding of the path being traveled and the challenges that lie ahead. They require preparation and thoughtful planning about the challenges to be overcome. Challenges are about opportunity. They are where the adventure begins and the inspiration for what makes a great journey, great.

Oddly enough, many couples don't take the time to adequately prepare, plan and understand the journey they are about to begin. They hear about the challenges that others have experienced, but pray that they will somehow avoid those same challenges. In other words, they want a journey without adventure. When the challenges do come, they view them as a reason to stop the journey instead of an opportunity to make the journey great.

Webster provides the following definition of a journey: "Something suggesting travel or passage from one place to another." As we travel from one place to another, the challenges we encounter often require a bridge. This bridge rests over impassable terrain and connects two parts of a singular journey and will help us overcome the challenge that would exist if the bridge wasn't there. The challenge does not disappear, it is overcome. Many couples need a bridge in their relationship. They need to overcome what they view as impassable terrain. That terrain may include anger, resentment, poor communication, conflict, unforgiveness, a lack of desire, as well as many other challenges.

You are about to take a journey through a seven bridge marriage. Each bridge reflects one of the seven foundational attributes of God's relationship to mankind discussed above: humility, forgiveness, healing, patience, fellowship, purpose and celebration. A seven bridge marriage is one that reflects the great design God has for marriage by putting in place the bridges necessary to overcome the challenges a couple will encounter on their marriage journey. You will cross one bridge at a time. Some bridges will take longer than others. At the end of this journey, you will know how to build these bridges in your marriage, as well as in your relationship with God. It will be up to you to cross them.

Chapter 2: The Bridge of Humility

Humility is without a doubt a core principle in God's relationship with mankind. The very thought of the Creator taking the form of the created in order to draw us back into a relationship with him is mind-boggling. Through this one act, God modeled for us that relationships are worth it at all costs. When we begin to get our minds around the concept that a marriage is a reflection of God's relationship to mankind, we must accept that humility must be a core principle in marriage. Even in the beginning when God created Adam and Eve, he did it in a way that brought the concept of humility into the relationship. In Genesis 2, God defines a part of marriage as Adam and Eve becoming one. We will explore the concept of being one further in the Bridge of Fellowship. But for now, it is important to consider that to become one, we have to deny our absolute individuality. This requires humility. The lack of humility breeds selfishness and self centeredness. When you think that you are more important than your spouse it will lead to bitterness and resentment in a marriage. Scripture says we are to "love others more than ourselves," which goes against the way the world typically functions. But we are called to be "in the world, not of the world."

Humility is also a foundation upon which many of the other Bridges are built. It is hard to forgive without humility. Patience often requires that we put our own agenda aside, which requires humility. Being open to a Purpose that might not be what you want also requires humility.

Andrew Murray, a South African minister, said that "Humility, the place of entire dependence on God, is from the very nature of things the first duty and the highest virtue of the creature, and the very root of every virtue. And so pride, or the loss of this humility, is the root of every sin and evil." He also said that "the root of all virtue and grace, of all faith and acceptable worship, is that we know that we have nothing but what we receive, and bow in deepest humility to wait upon God for it."

What is Humility

There are many misconceptions about humility. It is often described as some degree of super modesty or an unwillingness to accept praise. This however is not an accurate view of humility. Modesty and an unwillingness to accept praise are hardly the ingredients for a powerful force within a relationship. So let's explore humility. We view humility as being comprised of three primary attributes:

1. Healthy spiritual character
2. Genuine focus on others
3. Daily decision

Healthy spiritual character

Let's begin by exploring a great story found in 2 Chronicles 12 about Israel under the rule of King Rehoboam. This passage describes a time after King Rehoboam had become king of Israel and he had become a strong ruler. At this point it says that he abandoned the law of the Lord and the people of Israel followed him. In many respects it reflects a common pitfall that many of us face that when times are going well we tend to lose our spiritual focus. When our guard is let down we often allow outside influences to creep into our lives. In a similar way, this passage says that because he abandoned the law of the Lord, God allowed Israel to be attacked by King Shishak of Egypt. Egypt sent a powerful force and captured all of the cities of Judah and came up to Jerusalem.

At this point, the prophet Shemaiah met with King Rehoboam and other Israeli leaders and said, "This is what the Lord says: You have abandoned me, so I am abandoning you to Shishak." An interesting thing happened at this point. Unlike the way many people respond when confronted, they didn't make any excuses and they didn't try to justify themselves. We see a group of leaders that likely looked around the room at themselves, hung their heads and let out a self-reflective sigh. It says that the leaders of Israel and the king humbled themselves and said, "The Lord is right in doing this to us!"

Their humble response reflected a healthy spiritual character. They essentially said that God is greater than we are and is just, so we will subject ourselves to his direction and perspective. Their humility was demonstrated by acknowledging God's justice and not trying to justify their actions and complain about the result.

This is a great example of a healthy spiritual character. It does not describe someone that is perfect, but does describe someone that puts themselves in the right perspective before God and is willing to admit when they are wrong. We all make mistakes. The power of humility occurs in how we respond to the times when our mistakes are revealed.

Another great take away from this passage is the impact that their healthy spiritual character had on God's decision. It says that when God saw their change in heart he said, "Since the people have humbled themselves, I will not completely destroy them and will soon give them some relief. I will not use Shishak to pour out my anger on Jerusalem. But they will become his subjects, so that they will know the difference between serving me and serving earthly rulers."

Humility has the power to change the inevitable. It can soften hearts and create an environment where relationships can heal and grow again. This passage also brings up another point. You will be humbled one way or the other. You can either choose to be humble up front and live in peace, or be forced into humility and live in turmoil.

Genuine Focus on Others

The second aspect of humility is a genuine focus on others. Let's take a look at Philippians 2:3-5:

"Do nothing out of selfish ambition or vain conceit, but in humility consider others better than yourselves. Each of you should look not only to your own interests, but also the interests of others. Your attitude should be the same as that of Christ Jesus."

We'll talk about the attitude of Christ in a moment, but let's start with the first part of this passage. In the original Greek, this passage carries a meaning similar to how one would respond to others based on military rank. It reflects a behavior that does not act in your own self-interest, but shows respect and courtesy. You recognize that you are not the center of your universe, but are part of something much bigger. You yield to a common goal that protects and benefits you and those around you.

It is important to highlight that this passage does not suggest that humility means that you *believe* others are better than you. It says that we are to *consider* others better. So what is the difference? When you consider others better than yourself, your behavior reveals a different perspective. Your behavior treats others with respect and demonstrates a willingness to serve without reward. Your actions are so free of selfishness that it comes across that you think others are more important.

This was the attitude of Christ. Christ did not believe that he was better than everyone else. But he did come across that way in his behavior and attitude. Christ's attitude was that he came to serve. Mark 10:45 says, *"For even the Son of Man did not come to be served, but to serve, and give his life as a ransom for many."*

This passage in Philippians 2:3-5 is so powerful that we have to ask what a marriage would look like if it applied this principle. How would a husband and wife respond to each other and their children if their behavior and attitude reflected this type of humility?

<u>Daily Decision</u>

The final point in understanding humility is found in 1 Peter 5:5. It says that we are to "clothe" ourselves with humility. Why is this important? It is important because it suggests that humility is not something we are born with or forced into by others. Other people can humiliate us, but they can't humble us. Humility is a decision to act and approach life a certain way. It is not something that comes natural by any means, but it is something we should intentionally decide to do everyday just like getting dressed. In other words, it is not a natural part of us, but it should feel unnatural to walk out without it.

Why Humility is Important

When we read through scripture, we see four key reasons why humility is important in a relationship.

1. It allows God to teach us
2. It breaks down barriers of opposition
3. It allows us to create an atmosphere of peace
4. It allows us to make wise decisions

<u>Allows God to Teach Us</u>

I (Brian) remember when I started to teach our son to hit a baseball. When we first started, he exclaimed with confidence "I know how to do it!" He didn't believe that he needed to be taught. I decided to honor his confident spirit and threw the ball. A perfect strike! After a few more strikes I noticed that our son's confident spirit was beginning to ease. Not wanting him to get discouraged, I told him some stories about when I was learning to play baseball and how tough it was to learn to hit a ball that seemed to be flying at warp speed. A funny thing began to happen. He started to ask questions! How do I know when to swing? How do I hold the bat? How do I swing faster? He found humility and a willingness to be taught. He learned that it was okay to not know all the answers.

Psalm 25:9 says that God *"guides the humble in what is right and teaches them his way."* It is amazing how often we have heard couples say something like "My spouse just doesn't know me!" or "I don't know how to be married." At this point, we often point them to this passage and explain a simple concept: God knit your spouse together in the womb. He created your spouse and knows everything about them. If you want to know your spouse or learn how to be married to them, isn't it wise to ask the one that created them? If you're humble, then God can teach you how to relate to and understand your spouse. He can teach you how to reach their heart. You need to pray, "Lord, give me the keys to my spouse's heart!"

Breaks Down Barriers of Opposition

In James 4:6, it says that *"God opposes the proud, but gives grace to the humble."* This same principle exists within any relationship. It is pride that stops you from saying, "I'm sorry" and often prevents the necessary healing for a relationship to mend. When a relationship lacks humility, it creates barriers to true intimacy. We are often asked by couples how they can become more intimate. The answer is simple. Focus on humility. Jesus provided us with a great example of humility when he washed the disciples' feet during the Last Supper. Christ's humility reached into the hearts of the disciples and gave them the strength to get through some of the most difficult times of their lives which were soon to come.

Create an Atmosphere of Peace

Wouldn't it be nice to have abundant peace in your home and marriage? Psalm 37:11 says that the *"humble will inherent the earth and delight in abundant peace."* This type of peace is more than just a lack of conflict. A good old fashioned conflict is healthy for a marriage now and then. It brings forth your passions. The key is learning how to handle conflict when it arises so that it is fruitful.

All too often, we approach conflict in marriage with the sole objective of winning the argument. This "win at all cost" attitude will ultimately prove destructive over time in your marriage. Conflict should be viewed as a time where different perspectives are brought into a conversation. The goal should not be to win, but instead to be heard. Conflicts should not be rushed. It takes time for each person to ultimately feel as if the other person as really heard and understood them. It takes humility to step back and decide that you are willing to actually put your mouth on mute so that you can listen to your spouse. Conflicts tend to de-escalate quickly when the participants realize that each side is actually willing to listen.

When you approach your marriage with this type of humility, you can experience conflict and still delight in abundant peace.

Allows Us to Make Wise Decisions
The final reason why humility is so important in a marriage is found in Proverbs 11:2. It says that "with humility comes wisdom." Many couples make unwise decisions that later get them into trouble and cause stress in their relationship. These poor decisions are often rooted in a lack of humility, particularly as it relates to finances. We have seen many young couples that stretch themselves financially very early in their marriage. They soon begin to take on more and more debt in order to live an unrealistic lifestyle. This is often driven by pride or peer pressure. One of our favorite quotes is from Dave Ramsey, a financial talk show host. He often says that everyone is trying to keep up with the Jones', but they don't realize the Jones' are broke!

We encourage couples to practice a concept we call *Financial Humility*. Whenever you develop a family budget, buy a car or a house, or go on vacation, ask yourself if you are demonstrating financial humility. This doesn't mean that you can't buy a nice car or house, or go on a nice vacation. It means that you should ask yourself the motives behind your purchases. Make sure that they are not based on pride, arrogance or because you are trying to match the spending habits of others.

The results of unwise decisions rarely disappear quietly. They often require much effort and energy that could be spent in much more productive ways. As you and your spouse make decisions, ask yourselves if the choice you are able to make is based in humility or pride. This one question can prevent many future stresses in your marriage.

What Hinders Humility

Learning to practice humility in your relationships is a very challenging task. As we mentioned earlier, humility is not a natural part of us. Our human nature is not based on humility. We naturally tend to focus our attention on ourselves before others. This challenge can be overcome, but it is fought on three battlegrounds: Arrogance, Pride and Selfish Ambition.

The Battleground of Arrogance

Arrogance is about believing you are better than others. It is an attitude where one believes their greatness is so unique and that it is self-developed providing no credit to God or others. Proverbs 18:12 says *"Before destruction the heart of a man is haughty, but humility goes before honor."* When your heart is haughty or arrogant, there is no room for humility. An arrogant heart is often revealed through condescending words about others. It sends arrows that pierce the soul of others leaving wounds that are often carried for many years. The destruction that comes with arrogance often impacts many areas of life, including your marriage, job, friendships and relationship with God.

Battleground of Pride

Proverbs 29:23 says that *"Pride ends in humiliation, while humility brings honor."* Pride occurs when we seek self-focused pleasure. The Hebrew word for pride in this verse is Ga'avah which is the same word that describes the rising up or swelling of the sea. A wave in the sea only rises when it takes water away from other areas of the sea. It reminds us of the horrible tsunami that occurred on December 26, 2004 in the Indian Ocean, which killed more than 225,000 people in eleven countries. As the tsunami approached it pulled the shoreline water out to sea exposing an ocean floor that is normally below deep water. Moments later a wall of water with waves of up to 100 feet high crashed ashore. The impact was devastating. When one is prideful in their marriage, they take away from their spouse (or children) in order to focus on their own needs. One can only take for so long. It is important to remember that a wave always returns to sea level.

Battleground of Selfish Ambition

Harry Chapman wrote a song in 1974 called "Cats in the Cradle." It describes a father that is always too busy with his selfish ambition to spend time with his son. Although his son kept asking to spend time with him, he responded that he was too busy and they would spend time together soon. Later in life when things slow down for the father in his retirement, he wants to spend time with his son. Unfortunately, he finds that his son has become just like him and is now too busy for him with promises that they will get together soon. It is a sad reflection of a reality in today's society.

Philippians 2:3 calls us to do *"nothing out of selfish ambition."* When our focus is to succeed for our own glory, we destroy relationships. We become so self-focused that we ignore the needs of others, and our ambition is solely for the purpose of feeling good about ourselves.

What Promotes Humility

While humility is not a natural part of us, scripture provides us with a very clear indication of what promotes it in our lives. There are four key principles that help promote humility:

1. Trusting God
2. Praising God

3. Being obedient to God's word
4. Serving others

Trusting God

In Deuteronomy 8:16 it says that God gave the Israelites manna to eat while they were in the desert in order to humble and test them so that it would go well with them. The Israelites had to learn to trust God for his provision. That trust built humility because they focused on God's provision each day and not on their own efforts. It created a spiritual character in the Israelites as they began to see themselves in relation to God. The humility they developed through trust was what ultimately got them to the Promised Land.

It is important for couples to regularly ask themselves ways in which they are currently trusting on God. When couples start going through the motions of everyday life without maintaining a perspective about the ways God is guiding their steps, they often find themselves looking solely to each other for their needs to be met instead of God. God gave Eve to Adam in order to help him, not to meet his needs. God always wants us to look to him first to meet our needs. Our spouse plays a significant role, but that is more of a by-product than the primary purpose of why God puts them in our life.

Praising God

The next three principles to promote humility can be found in Philippians 2:5-8 where Paul describes Christ's humility and points to several aspects of his attitude that created his humble spirit.

He first brings in the concept of praising God. When you praise God, it allows you to recognize your lowliness relative to his greatness. Through praise, we focus on his power, love, faithfulness, and holiness. We see that we are incapable of equality with God and are only left with the ability to praise him. We find this principle in Philippians 2:6, where it says that Christ "did not see equality *with God as something to be grasped.*" Our spiritual character is often developed during the times we praise God.

Serving Others

In Philippians 2:7, Paul presents another principle in the development of humility. He says that Christ took the very nature of a servant. Serving others involves putting ourselves in a more vulnerable position. It brings perspective and a dose of humility into almost any situation as it takes the focus off of you and toward others. For the past several years, we have worked with a local ministry before Thanksgiving to make baskets of food to be delivered to less fortunate families. The baskets of food are comprised of food that has been donated from throughout the community. We have always been blessed with a full Thanksgiving dinner table with all the traditional trimmings. The first time we helped make these baskets, we realized how much we had taken our fortune for granted. It is very easy to overlook some of God's most basic blessings. When we serve, those blessings emerge from the darkness and allow you to experience God's blessings again in a new and powerful way. It truly is an experience in humility. It is very hard to complain that your Thanksgiving turkey is a little dry after that experience. Look for opportunities to serve and not only will your humility grow, but you will further experience the joys of God's blessings in your life.

Being Obedient to God's Word

In Philippians 2:8, we find the forth principle that encourages humility. It says that Christ "*humbled himself and became obedient to death on the cross.*" God asks for our obedience to his word. When we are obedient to God, we acknowledge that his ways are better than ours and we are willing to be led by him. Conversely, our disobedience suggests that we believe that our ways are better than Gods. Is the created greater than the Creator? By spending time understanding God's word and practicing obedience, we will begin to develop greater humility.

It is amazing how many Christians express feelings of such defeat in this area. They describe feelings of such anger at themselves whenever they stumble. We don't believe God wants obedience to be an easy thing. If it was then we wouldn't even think about it and would likely become prideful in our obedience. Obedience is developed and learned over time. Hebrews 5:8 says that Christ *"learned obedience from what he suffered."* If Christ had to learn obedience, then how much more do we? When you feel disappointment in your shortcomings, praise God! Isn't it a good thing to regret our disobedience as opposed to being apathetic? As you learn obedience, you will also learn humility.

How Humility is Demonstrated by God

There is no better way to understand humility than to read all the ways it is demonstrated by God throughout scripture. In Matthew 11:29 Christ says, *"Take my yoke upon you and learn from me, for I am gentle and humble in heart, and you will find rest for your souls."* Christ described himself as humble in heart. The Greek word for heart in this verse is *kardia* which describes the center of one's physical and spiritual life, including the senses, soul, mind, will and character. He viewed humility as the central expression of who he was and he wanted to share that with others. Christ didn't just want to go around preaching, but instead wanted to change our lives for the better. He wanted us to experience a life with fewer burdens. It is a great lesson for us to apply in the home. Do we spend more time increasing or easing the burdens on our family?

One of the most powerful depictions of humility is found in John 13. Here we find Christ and the disciples at the Last Supper. As the meal was being served, Jesus got up and began to wash the disciples' feet. The idea alone of the Messiah washing the feet of his disciples reflects an astonishing level of humility. How many leaders today in business, politics, and even the family treat others with such dignity? However, the most astonishing part of Christ's actions was not just that he washed the disciples' feet, but that he washed the feet of Judas, his betrayer. Later in the meal, Jesus told Judas to go do what he needed to do. How easy would it have been for Christ to stop as he arrived to Judas' feet and release him to go at that point? Instead, it was an expression of how God is willing to clean each one of us despite our sinfulness. Are you willing to wash your spouse's feet when they are at their worst? God set an example for us to be willing to demonstrate humility in our actions even when we feel justified to do the opposite.

Jesus was able to demonstrate this level of humility because he kept a perspective that he was here to serve and do the will of God. He did not have any interest in the praise or recognition of men. Throughout his ministry he focused on God alone. In John 14:10 Jesus said, "Don't you believe that I am in the Father, and that the Father is in me? The words I say to you are not just my own. Rather, it is the Father, living in me, who is doing his work." He recognized that everything he did and said was based on the power of God. This perspective was important from the beginning of his ministry as it is the exact area where Satan tried to tempt him in Luke 4:1-13. It is important to continually keep our perspective focused on God. When we lose that perspective, it makes us more vulnerable to temptation and the things that hinder humility.

How Humility is Demonstrated in Marriage
Learning to practice humility can often feel like a daunting task. We have found that it helps to think about humility in the following categories. Once we understand some practical ways to practice humility, we often find it is a quality that grows over time.

Leadership
Every home needs leadership. We find that many couples struggle with the concept of spiritual leadership. They tend to understand that it is needed in the relationship, but they express some frustration that it has become more of a buzzword and find little guidance on what it is. Spiritual leadership is about demonstrating humility and putting the needs of your family first. It is about serving everyone else in the family. Leadership in the home is not about making decisions and getting your way. It is a daily demonstration that the needs of your

family are your greatest priority. We find this principle in Mark 9:35 when it says that *"Sitting down, Jesus called the Twelve and said, 'If anyone wants to be first, he must be the very last, and the servant of all.'"* Jesus said this right after the disciples were arguing about who was the greatest. Great husbands, wives, fathers and mothers learn that leading through service and putting the needs of others before themselves creates an atmosphere of peace, love and spiritual growth. Are you willing to cancel your weekly golf outing when the house is a mess so that you can serve in the home and help your spouse?

Keep Your Promises

Romans 15:8 says, *"For I tell you that Christ has become a servant of the Jews on behalf of God's truth, to confirm the promises made to the patriarchs."* God's promises are unwavering. He does not break his promises and was willing to become a servant through Christ in order to fulfill his promises. It took great humility to choose to become a servant for a people that would turn their backs on him. However, God knew that the outcome was more important that his stature among the people. Likewise, we need to view a healthy marriage relationship as the most important outcome. Be a servant to your spouse and keep your promises, even when it hurts. When we break our promises, it is often a result of other selfish motives. Also, be careful not to make promises that you know you can't keep.

Limit Your Wants

Conflicts within a relationship often result from pure selfishness. We want something and don't get it. James 4:1-2 says, *"What causes fights and quarrels among you? Don't they come from your desires that battle within you? You want something but don't get it. You kill and covet, but you cannot have what you want. You quarrel and fight. You do not have, because you do not ask God."* Demonstrate humility by focusing less on your personal wants and more on the needs of your spouse. This of course needs to be balanced such that one spouse doesn't become a doormat to the demands of their spouse.

Apologize

2 Corinthians 7:9-10 says, *"yet now I am happy, not because you were made sorry, but because your sorrow led you to repentance. For you became sorrowful as God intended and so were not harmed in any way by us. Godly sorrow brings repentance that leads to salvation and leaves no regret, but worldly sorrow brings death."* It is important to distinguish between an apology due to godly sorrow and worldly sorrow. Worldly sorrow occurs when we feel bad that we were caught. Godly sorrow recognizes that we failed to live up to the standards of God and desire to deny ourselves and not do it again. This takes humility. Be willing to say you're sorry to your spouse. Not just to avoid them getting angry, but because you recognize that your spouse deserves your best efforts. You committed yourself to a high standard of love and honor with your wedding vows. Be willing to live up to those standards.

Patience

Ecclesiastes 7:8 says that *"patience is better than pride."* Patience reflects a level of humility that acknowledges that our time table and our agenda is not the highest priority. When we are patient with our spouse, we say that we care enough for them to put our immediate desires on hold. We will spend more time discussing patience under the Bridge of Patience.

Giving

The act of giving (with honest intent) is based in part on humility. It is a result of focusing on the needs of others. It requires that we deny something for ourselves, whether it is our time, energy or resources, and use that to provide for someone else. 1 Chronicles 29:17 says, *"I know, my God, that you test the heart and are pleased with integrity. All these things have I given willingly and with honest intent. And now I have seen with joy how willingly your people who are here have given to you."* We believe that the act of giving can have a dramatic impact on a relationship if a couple makes a list of 5 things that can each give up in order to give to their spouse. Then over the course of the next 6-12 months, put it into practice. You will be encouraged by the results.

Steps toward Humility

Once we develop a greater understanding of the concept of humility, it is important to put it into practice. However, this can be a challenging task. How does one focus on developing a trait that in many respects is about not focusing on yourself! The following steps should help you in making humility a part of your daily life.

Fasten It

Earlier we looked at the passage in 1 Peter 5:5 which says we are to clothe ourselves in humility. We must decide to practice humility every day. It is very easy to lose sight of it once you walk out of the house and begin your daily routine. It must be intentional and fastened to decisions and actions. Be proactive and look for opportunities to demonstrate humility and look towards the interest of your spouse and others. In many respects, this can feel rather awkward especially if you feel disingenuous. That is not unusual and should be expected. You are choosing to practice something that is not natural. Make a list of acts of humility that you could do during the week. Start small. It could be as simple as taking out the garbage or cleaning up the kitchen. Once you begin to choose some simple acts of humility, you will find it easier to make them a daily part of your life.

Believe It

One of the many hurdles in practicing humility comes from a lack of perceived benefit. Why should I do something when it will never benefit me? Why should I be the one to compromise my time, energy and resources? In 1 Peter 5:6, we are told that God promises to lift up those that humble themselves. Count on this promise as a way to cast out the fear that you are compromising yourself. Remember as Mary proclaimed in Luke 1:52 that God has "*brought down the rulers from their thrones and lifted up the humble.*" This is great news if we believe it. We have found that many couples that are undergoing struggles often find themselves in a stalemate with their spouse. Both have been offended by the other. They want to restore the relationship, but neither is willing to make the first move. They fear making the first move, because it may show a weakness that will later be exploited. Sadly, many of these relationships take their stalemate to the courthouse. Humility often requires that you make the first move. When you do this, remember that the Lord is the one that will lift you up, not necessarily your spouse. Make your move, but look to the promises of God.

Cast It

Humility requires that you deny yourself, which requires that you cast off the sins that hold you captive in selfishness. James 1:21 says, "*Therefore, get rid of all moral filth and the evil that is so prevalent and humbly accept the word planted in you, which can save you.*" You must identify any recurring sins that are rooted in selfishness and pray continuously to overcome the stronghold. As you begin to cast off the sins in your life, you will experience the grace of God that draws your focus to him. With that focus, you will find it easier to practice humility.

Take It

The final step towards humility is also a daily choice. In Luke 9:23 Christ said "*If anyone would come after me, he must deny himself and take up his cross daily and follow me.*" By taking up our cross daily, we maintain an awareness of the need to forgive others and focus on the Kingdom of God. We maintain this awareness because our personal cross reflects the punishment we deserve for our sins. Christ allowed himself to be punished on our personal cross. Once we grasp the reality of his actions, it is very difficult to cast stones at others. This awareness creates humility and is a foundation in the maintenance and healing of healthy relationships.

Summary

Micah 6:8 says that the Lord requires us to "act justly, love mercy and walk humbly with God." Acting justly and loving mercy are personal actions and attributes. Walking humbly defines the nature of our relationship with God. God wants our daily walk with him to be based on humility. In the same way, we need to walk humbly with our spouse. Remember that humility is a choice. It is a decision that you make about how you want to view and respond to others. If you make the decision to practice humility, then you will begin to establish the foundation necessary to build a healthy marriage.

Bridge of Humility: Study Questions

What is Humility

How would you describe God's perspective?

How would you describe your perspective?

What would your actions suggest is the most important thing to you?

How would someone with a lower rank respond to others?

What would a marriage look like if the husband and wife both applied the principles in Philippians 2:3-5?

When is it difficult to act in humility toward others?

Why Humility is Important

Why is humility an important part of being teachable?

What would you like to learn about your spouse?

What are some things you do that causes your spouse to "oppose" you?

What are some ways you could give grace to your spouse?

In what areas do we experience a lack of peace in our relationship?

How could humility help our relationship experience peace in those areas?

Why do you think humility makes us wiser?

What are some areas in your relationship where you would like more wisdom?

What Hinders Humility

Are there any ways that we talk about others in a condescending way?

What are some cures for arrogance?

What are some ways that a couple could compete against each other?

What are the differences between good and bad ambition?

What are some ways that selfish ambition can harm a family?

What Promotes Humility

What are some ways that trust is built and broken?

What are some ways that we can praise God?

When do you feel closest to God?

What are some areas where it is difficult to be obedient?

What are some ways that we can serve others together?

How Humility is Demonstrated by God

What are some of the areas where we can make humility our central focus?

How have you demonstrated humility in the last year?

What are some new ways you can serve your spouse?

What are some ways to keep your perspective focused on God?

How Humility is Demonstrated in Marriage

Why do you think serving is such an important aspect of leadership?

What are some ways you could lead by being last?

What promises have been difficult for you to keep and why?

What arguments do we have that are a result of us not getting what we want?

Do you find it difficult or easy to apologize and why?

What are some things you would like to apologize for?

What are some ways patience can create thankfulness in a marriage?

What are some things that your spouse would like for you to give them?

Steps to Humility

What is the most difficult area to look to the interest of others?

What are some ways that would help keep humility on the forefront of your mind?

What are some ways that being humble can benefit you later?

Why do you think that recurring sin prevents humility?

In what ways did Christ's sinless life help him demonstrate humility?

What are some ways that you can take up your cross daily?

Chapter 3: The Bridge of Forgiveness

Previously, we discussed how marriage is a journey. In many respects, this journey is not found in any greater way than in the process of forgiveness. Forgiveness often requires time and is one of the most important aspects of a healthy relationship. Forgiveness either strengthens or weakens the bond between individuals. It is also something that every person will be confronted with throughout their lifetime. One's perspective on forgiveness not only impacts the health of their relationships, but also their own emotional, physical and spiritual health.

As we have counseled and mentored couples over the years, we are no longer surprised when we find that issues surrounding forgiveness tend to be focal points in their relationship struggles. These issues are not always even directly a result of unforgiveness towards a spouse, but instead are related to other relationships and the result of unforgiveness manifests itself in the marriage. Often, the issues surrounding forgiveness are not obvious right away. It is not uncommon that they get buried over many years and are not even known to exist.

Forgiveness is also not a straight forward issue. Questions such as "Have I really forgiven someone?" or "What does it mean to forgive?" are not uncommon. Forgiveness is also the central theme of the ministry of Jesus Christ and our relationship to God. It is the glue that binds us to the heart of God and secures our eternity in heaven. That is pretty important and commands our attention to truly understand it in our lives. As we begin to talk about forgiveness, let's keep the following principles in mind: (1) All have sinned and fallen short of the glory of God and (2) Do unto others as you would have them do unto you.

What is Forgiveness

One misconception about forgiveness is that is has no accountability. That is, many people struggle with forgiveness because they believe that it means that the person being forgiven is getting off "scott-free." This couldn't be further from the truth. We describe it as atonement and a release.

<u>Atonement</u>
Hebrews 9:22 says, "*In fact, the law requires that nearly everything be cleansed with blood and without the shedding of blood there is no forgiveness.*" Scripture is very clear that forgiveness does not happen without the shedding of blood, just as Christ had to shed his blood. In other words, forgiveness requires atonement. This should alleviate the concerns of those that struggle with whether there should be some accountability for the hurtful action of others. The key is to understand the nature of atonement.

> *In him we have redemption through his blood, the forgiveness of sins, in accordance with the riches of God's grace.*
>
> - *Ephesians 1:7*

> *God presented Christ as a sacrifice of atonement through the shedding of his blood —to be received by faith. He did this to demonstrate his righteousness, because in his forbearance he had left the sins committed beforehand unpunished — he did it to demonstrate his righteousness at the present time, so as to be just and the one who justifies those who have faith in Jesus.*
>
> - *Romans 3:25-26*

The crucifixion of Jesus was the atonement for <u>all</u> sins. That means, when your spouse sins against you, the atonement has already been made by the crucifixion. That is a very difficult concept for many people to accept and even more difficult to remember in the heat of an argument! When we are wronged, we often want to be the one that holds people accountability through some form of retribution or punishment. It could be the silent treatment, harsh words, or even physical aggression. However, one of the greatest things about the atonement of the crucifixion is that it frees us from the burden of accountability. I basically recognize that I have been sinned against, but am willing to accept that

Christ's atonement is sufficient and I no longer have an obligation to seek further punishment. Forgiveness is an act of faith!

Release

Once we understand that forgiveness comes about because of and after atonement, we then must understand what happens at the point of forgiveness. It is at this point that we have a role and a responsibility.

If we look at Numbers 14:19-20, the Lord says that he would *"forgive the sin of these people, just as he pardoned them from the time they left Egypt."* The word for pardon in Hebrew is *Calach* which means both to pardon and forgive. Think of what happens in a presidential pardon. A pardon is both the forgiveness of a crime and the penalty associated with it.

In Hebrews 10:17-18, God says, *"Their sins and lawless acts I will remember no more." And where these have been forgiven, there is no longer any sacrifice for sin.*

There are 2 great points here. First, the Greek word for "remember" in this verse is *Mimnesko,* which is a verb meaning to recall or to return to one's mind. It reflects an active process of *wanting* to recall an event. Have you ever had a hard time letting something go? You keep thinking about and pondering an issue. You want to remember it so you dwell on it. You may even rehearse how you will respond to the situation when you get the next chance. This is often a result of anger which we will discuss later in more detail.

The second point is that once something has been forgiven, it is no longer possible to make atonement. This is a difficult, but important concept. Christ was the sacrifice; therefore, there is no additional sacrifice needed or available. Think about the concept of "double jeopardy," which doesn't allow someone to be tried again for the same crime. What has been atoned has been atoned. If I try to punish someone further, then I am essentially saying that Christ's death on the cross wasn't good enough. I put myself in the place of God as judge and say that I can make a better determination of an acceptable punishment, because what God did through Christ didn't go far enough. Think about the arrogance of such a concept. This also shows why the Bridge of Humility is an important part of forgiveness.

So let's put this in the context of everyday life. Your spouse does something that is clearly wrong. It hurts you and angers you. There are two responses. You can hold onto that anger and punish them by yelling at them, giving them the silent treatment, making them feel that they owe you something and have to make up for what they did wrong. When you respond this way, you are striving to do in the flesh, what has already been done in the spirit.

Or you can say, OK, they messed up. Christ has made atonement for their actions. It is not my responsibility to punish them since Christ took the punishment. My responsibility is to demonstrate the forgiving power of Christ by showing mercy and grace to my spouse. I will release myself from the burden of feeling that I have an obligation to punish them. What they did was not okay, but I am okay.

Romans 12:19-21 says, "*Do not take revenge, my friends, but leave room for God's wrath, for it is written: "It is mine to avenge; I will repay," says the Lord. On the contrary: If your enemy is hungry, feed him; if he is thirsty, give him something to drink. In doing this, you will heap burning coals on his head. Do not be overcome by evil, but overcome evil with good.*"

Okay, cut yourself some slack, though. We all have those shining moments when we lose it and snap back at our spouse. The point is to have the right perspective about forgiveness and work towards it as quickly as you can. Now we have talked about what forgiveness is, now let's focus a little bit on why it is so essential in a relationship....especially a marriage.

Why Forgiveness is Important

Learning to forgive properly is so important to our emotional, physical and spiritual health. When we harbor unforgiveness, it negatively impacts all areas of our lives.

<u>Commanded</u>

The primary reason that we are to forgive is that we are commanded to do it in all relationships. We believe that a marriage relationship has even greater importance since it is God's chosen reflection of his relationship to mankind. By not readily forgiving your spouse, you distort the picture of God's relationship to us and tear apart God's design for marriage.

Matthew 6:14-15 says, "*For if you forgive men when they sin against you, your heavenly Father will also forgive you. But if you do not forgive men their sins, your Father will not forgive your sins.*" Christ made this statement immediately after giving the disciples the Lord's Prayer where he also stressed the need of forgiving others.

Consider the following passages on forgiveness:

"*Then Peter came to Jesus and asked, "Lord, how many times shall I forgive my brother when he sins against me? Up to seven times?" Jesus answered, "I tell you, not seven times, but seventy-seven times.*

-   *Matthew 18:21-22*

"*And when you stand praying, if you hold anything against anyone, forgive him, so that your Father in heaven may forgive you your sins.*"

-   *Mark 11:25*

Our obligation to forgive is clearly commanded in scripture. We often do not like to hear the harshness of this requirement, but it is a clear message of Christ. If we accept the forgiveness of our sins by God, then we must demonstrate that same willingness to forgive others that have sinned against us.

If you look at the parable of the unmerciful servant in Matthew 18, it is hard to misinterpret the message. The parable in Matthew 18 describes the unmerciful servant and the fact that he was turned over to the torturers. People that don't forgive are often tormented by the anger and resentment that slowly builds up in their heart. This often leads to sickness and disease, and has been linked to mental depression, high blood pressure, heart disease, and even substance abuse.

Another reason that forgiveness on our part is important is that it keeps our focus on the saving grace of Christ. We recognize that God is a perfect judge and we have no obligations beyond his perfect judgment. This is a matter of respecting God's authority and demonstrating our humility. Remember, it is up to the other person to accept your forgiveness. You are just commanded to forgive.

Recognition

When we offer immediate and unconditional forgiveness, we demonstrate our recognition that God is the judge of all sin, and we are not putting ourselves in the place of overriding God's perfect judgment. We are not to determine the punishment of those that sin against us. That right is given to God alone. Psalm 50:6 says, "*And the heavens proclaim his righteousness, for he is a God of justice.*" Further, Acts 10:42 says, "*He commanded us to preach to the people and to testify that he is the one whom God appointed as judge of the living and the dead.*"

Now, it is not a point of contention in the church that God is our judge. That is pretty much universally accepted. However, it is not uncommon that we treat God's justice as that of a lower court judge and we reserve the right for ourselves to sit as a judge on the Supreme Court to render our own opinion as to whether the prior ruling of God was sufficient or reasonable.

The next time you feel the need to render a separate judgment, remember Romans 14:10 that says, *"You, then, why do you judge your brother or sister? Or why do you treat them with contempt? For we will all stand before God's judgment seat."*

Closeness

God makes us aware of salvation through the forgiveness of our sins. Once we become aware of the salvation available because of his forgiveness, it draws us close to him to accept that forgiveness through Christ. Similarly, the act of forgiveness by each one of us will draw others closer to us in a healthy relationship. It creates a greater ability and desire to show similar love to others.

Below is a great conversation between Jesus and Peter found in Luke 7:40-47 in which Jesus explains that when you are forgiven it creates a desire to show love and be close to the forgiver.

Jesus answered him, "Simon, I have something to tell you." "Tell me, teacher," he said. "Two people owed money to a certain moneylender. One owed him five hundred denarii and the other fifty. Neither of them had the money to pay him back, so he forgave the debts of both. Now which of them will love him more?"

Simon replied, "I suppose the one who had the bigger debt forgiven." "You have judged correctly," Jesus said.

Then he turned toward the woman and said to Simon, "Do you see this woman? I came into your house. You did not give me any water for my feet, but she wet my feet with her tears and wiped them with her hair. You did not give me a kiss, but this woman, from the time I entered, has not stopped kissing my feet. You did not put oil on my head, but she has poured perfume on my feet. Therefore, I tell you, her many sins have been forgiven—as her great love has shown. But whoever has been forgiven little loves little."

If your spouse does not feel close to you, ask yourself whether they feel forgiven by you. Do you make your spouse constantly have to prove themselves to you? Or, maybe you just haven't taken the time to embrace them and let them know that all is forgiven and they no longer have to win your approval.

Restoration

When we forgive others, we allow the restoration of a relationship to occur. Without forgiveness, restoration is not possible. In Romans 12:18, we are called to do our part to live at peace with everyone. This means that when a relationship has been torn, we need to do everything in our power to mend the relationship, which includes forgiveness.

This is not an easy thing to do. It is often much easier to be grumpy and wait for our spouse to come graveling back to us even when we share the blame for an argument. It takes a conscious effort to lay down our perceived "right" for some additional justice and to be willing to take the first step towards restoration. Relationships that last and are healthy are the ones in which each spouse recognizes their need to restore the relationship during periods of strife.

What Hinders Forgiveness

Harboring Offense

When we become offended and are unwilling to let go of that offense, we will be unable to offer forgiveness. When we hold onto our offenses, we will eventually become bitter and it will tear apart our relationships.

I have swept away your offenses like a cloud, your sins like the morning mist.
Return to me, for I have redeemed you.

- *Isaiah 44:22*

A person's wisdom yields patience; it is to one's glory to overlook an offense.

- *Proverbs 19:11*

We become offended when we believe that we are owed something and we do not receive what we are owed. Our expectations determine what we believe we are owed. For example, let's say that you expect that your spouse will call you if they will be more than 15 minutes late getting home for dinner at 6:00 pm. It is now 6:45 pm and you haven't heard a thing. The meal on the table is now cold, you haven't eaten yet and it is now time to get the kids ready for bed. At 7:00 pm, your spouse pulls into the driveway. Fireworks time! Do you have a right to be upset? Absolutely! Do you have a right to let your spouse know that you are upset? Absolutely! Do you have an obligation to then calm yourself down, let it go and forgive your spouse? Absolutely.

Anger

Ephesians 4:26-27 calls on us to resolve our anger quickly. When we hold onto our anger, we make it more difficult for us to forgive. The reason is that while we are angry, we begin to justify all the reasons that we are offended and why the other person was so wrong. As this list grows, we add more bricks in the walls that we put up between our relationships. This begins to separate the relationship over time, further increasing the challenge of forgiveness.

It is important to recognize that reconciliation and forgiveness can be a process, which may take time for ultimate resolution. However, Ephesians 4:26-27 is a call to immediately start that process. It calls us to get rid of our anger, which happens when we accept that Christ's atonement was sufficient.

Pride

The selfishness that is imbedded in pride is one of the greatest inhibitors to forgiveness. Pride causes problems in strained relationships in the same way as fuel to a fire. Pride can make our anger, bitterness and resentment grow rapidly and out of control.

In his pride the wicked man does not seek him; in all his thoughts there is no room for God.

- *Psalm 10:4*

Where there is strife there is pride, but wisdom is found in those who take advice.

- *Proverbs 13:10*

We need to see that we are just as guilty as everyone else (Romans 3:23) and we all have our own struggles. When we consider others better than ourselves as seen in Philippians 2:3, we recognize that our own sinfulness prevents us from looking down on others in their struggles. We need to be mindful of the log in our own eyes (Matthew 7:3). When we maintain a mindset of humility to prevent pride from ruling our actions, then we begin to allow ourselves to be open to forgiveness.

What Promotes Forgiveness

Humility

Forgiveness often requires our humility so that God can guide us through a difficult time of personal sacrifice. Psalm 25:9 says *"He guides the humble in what is right and teaches them his way."* When we are humble, we make ourselves teachable by God and allow his grace to work in our lives. God understands that his expectations for us to forgive are challenging, so he makes himself available to give us the strength and guidance to forgive others when we are hurt.

Finally, all of you, be like-minded, be sympathetic, love one another, be compassionate and humble.

- *1 Peter 3:8*

Humility also enables us to create an environment when we can live at peace with one another. Not only does it allow us to forgive, but it makes it easier for others to ask forgiveness without fear of condemnation. Romans 8:1 makes it clear that there is no condemnation for those that are in Christ Jesus. Humility allows us to give up the perceived right to offer our own condemnation of others, which has already been satisfied by the crucifixion.

Love

Numbers 14 talks about a time after the Israelites sent men to explore the land of Canaan, and they came back saying that even though it was all God promised, it was inhabited by people that would be too powerful to overcome. The Israelites immediately responded with anger and contempt for God and wanted to return to Egypt. This angered God to the point that he was prepared to strike them all down with a plague and destroy everyone except Moses, and restart the nation of Israel through Moses. However, because of God's love, he forgave them and didn't destroy them. Forgiveness requires love. It was because of God's love of mankind that he gave his son to die for our sins.

Couples that want to create an environment where forgiveness comes more naturally need to focus on creating an environment of love in their home. They need to learn how to show love for their spouse so that their spouse feels loved. It is not enough to just say I love my spouse if they don't feel it. We need to begin to express the kind of love described in 1 Corinthians 13.

Ephesians 5:22-23 is one of the most challenging passages in scripture. It makes a clear call to married couples to be imitators of God's relationship with mankind. Wives are called to respect the authority of their husbands in the same manner as they respect the authority of Christ. We respect Christ because we love him, recognizing what he has done for us. This command to be imitators of Christ also establishes an expectation that the husband should respond to that respect in the same manner as Christ does through his love of the church by his forgiveness.

<u>Repentance</u>

Repentance is an important part of forgiveness. Luke 3:3 says "*he went into all the country around Jordan, preaching baptism of repentance for the forgiveness of sins.*" Simply, repentance is the act of going in the opposite direction of our prior sinful actions. When we recognize our wrongs and demonstrate our sincerity about turning away from continuing those actions, it makes it easier for others to forgive us. At the same time, when we continue to do the same thing over and over, it makes it that much more difficult for your spouse to continually forgive.

Repent, then, and turn to God, so that your sins may be wiped out, that times of refreshing may come from the Lord.

- *Acts 3:19*

However, it is important to recognize that we are called to forgive in spite of others repentance. Their repentance is for their benefit as it allows them to accept the forgiveness being offered. It is not something that we should demand prior to our offer of forgiveness. Often times, forgiveness must occur first in order for others to feel love that leads to repentance.

How Forgiveness is Demonstrated by God

<u>Timing</u>

A misconception that many people have about forgiveness is that the person that caused the harm must say, "I'm sorry" before being forgiven. If we look at how God demonstrates forgiveness, we can gain a better appreciation for how we should also view our forgiveness of others.

You, Lord, are forgiving and good, abounding in love to all who call to you.

- *Psalm 86:5*

The Lord our God is merciful and forgiving, even though we have rebelled against him.

- *Daniel 9:9*

But God demonstrates his own love for us in this: While we were still sinners, Christ died for us.

- *Romans 5:8*

God by his very nature is forgiving. God's forgiveness was made "when you were dead in your sins." He did not wait until we said, "I'm sorry" before he made his forgiveness available through the atonement of Christ's death. His death on the cross made forgiveness immediately available. However, the acceptance of that forgiveness by the sinner is what is necessary for their salvation.

Compassion

The parable of the prodigal son in Luke 15 provides many insights into the relationship between God and mankind. One of the humbling points is the picture of the father (God) running to his son (mankind) before his son even spoke a word. It reveals the passion and willingness that God has to forgive and his desire to have fellowship with us. God runs to us with compassion and acceptance even before we say, "I'm sorry."

Do you offer that level of compassion to your spouse? Are you eager to embrace them before they say, or even if they don't say, I'm sorry? You have to decide what type of marriage you want. Will it look like the father racing to his son, or will it look like a father sitting on the porch with his arms crossed?

Delight

How often do we approach forgiveness grudgingly? We face internal torment trying to decide when we can gather the nerve to forgive and how to suppress our desire for retribution.   God, in contrast, delights in showing mercy through his forgiveness!

> *Who is God like you, who pardons sin and forgives the transgression of the remnant of his inheritance? You do not stay angry forever but delight to show mercy.*
>
> - *Micah 7:18*

When we are able to change our mindset so that we actually are excited about being able to forgive, we will then begin to experience the joy in all circumstances that God desires for each of us.

How Forgiveness is Demonstrated in Marriage

Acceptance

God forgave us because of the acceptable atonement of Christ's death on the cross; not because of any act of atonement on our part. 1 John 2:2 says *"He is the atoning sacrifice for our sins, and not only for ours but also for the sins of the whole world."*

The challenge placed before each of us is whether we are willing to accept the atonement that has been made for our spouse and others. If we accept that atonement, then we must forgive. Romans 15:7 says *"Accept one another, then, just as Christ accepted you, in order to bring praise to God."*

Jesus accepted each of us with our sin, because of the atonement that he made on our behalf. He calls each of us to then accept others based on the atonement that was already made for them.

Acceptance can be shown in many ways. Maybe it is a long warm hug, or maybe some flowers or a gift. How different is that from our typical approach? Think about it. The one that was sinned against is the one that presents flowers to their spouse and says, "I still love you." Instead, the path most often traveled waits for the sinning spouse to come back graveling with a gift in hand.

Comfort

Whenever we offer forgiveness, it is crucial that we handle that forgiveness appropriately. It should be a time of reconciliation and support of each other. It is very easy to take a selfish joy as we offer forgiveness and then watch the other person grieve. Here is a great passage that discusses this point.

> *If anyone has caused grief, he has not so much grieved me as he has grieved all of you to some extent—not to put it too severely. The punishment inflicted on him by the majority is sufficient. Now instead, you ought to forgive and comfort him, so that he will not be overwhelmed by excessive sorrow. I urge you, therefore, to reaffirm your love for him. Another reason I wrote you was to see if you would stand the test and be obedient in everything. Anyone you forgive, I also forgive. And what I have forgiven—if there was anything to forgive—I have forgiven in the sight of Christ for your sake, in order that Satan might not outwit us. For we are not unaware of his schemes.*
>
> - *2 Corinthians 2:5-11*

Once we forgive, we must be willing to then offer comfort to our spouse to let them know that our love for them has not wavered. We need to build each other up so that through our challenges we become stronger.

Grin and Bear It!

Forgiving is not always easy. Colossians 3:13 says *"Bear with each other and forgive one another if any of you has a grievance against someone. Forgive as the Lord forgave you."*

In Matthew 26:36-46, you find that even Christ struggled in the Garden of Gethsemane with walking to the cross. God never said that forgiving would be easy for us. Sometimes we just need to pray with the same passion as Christ and then show our obedience to the calling of God.

This should give you some relief! You don't have to be a super-human where forgiveness comes easy. It is allowed to be really hard, and it will be really hard. There will be times that you will need to spend plenty of time in prayer asking God to give you the strength to forgive. That is okay. The key is being willing to get to your knees in prayer so that God can soften your heart.

Don't Escalate

Escalation occurs when couples go back and forth with verbal assaults and each response is intended to show greater power. The result is a more hostile environment. James 1:19 calls us to be quick to listen, slow to speak and slow to become angry. Escalating an argument will only result in greater hurt for those involved. Galatians 5:15 says *"If you bite and devour each other, watch out or you will be destroyed by each other."*

It is amazing how often we are prone to escalate an argument. If you look back over all the times that one of your arguments escalated, how many of those times can you say that the escalation was beneficial? You might end up "winning" by beating down your spouse with verbal grenades, but at what cost? What is even more amazing is how often escalation occurs over really pointless issues. It takes a lot of patience and self-control to learn to not escalate an argument. Remember, escalations only occur when both parties participate, so you can't ever blame your spouse for escalation.

Steps to Forgiveness

Pray

Forgiveness often requires an inner strength that we are not able to reach on our own (Ephesians 3:16). God will provide the strength necessary to forgive if we ask him in prayer. We also need to go to God with sincerity. Be honest in your prayers with God. If you don't want to forgive, then let God know that and ask him to help you soften your heart.

Soften Your Heart

Whenever we allow our hearts to harden, we separate ourselves from God making it more difficult to forgive.

Blessed is the one who always trembles before God, but whoever hardens their heart falls into trouble.

- *Proverbs 28:14*

They are darkened in their understanding and separated from the life of God because of the ignorance that is in them due to the hardening of their hearts.

- *Ephesians 4:18*

Our hearts become hardened when we focus on our bitterness and anger. When we instead take the time to focus on the positive traits of the person(s) with whom we are angry, we will allow our hearts to soften. We need to see others as God sees them and remember that he was willing to forgive them.

Remember

When we take the time to remember that we are also sinners (Romans 3:23) and that Christ has forgiven us, it makes it easier to forgive others. In the parable of the unmerciful servant in Matthew 18:21-35, Jesus explains the importance of remembering our forgiveness and offering that same forgiveness towards others.

Before Jesus told the disciples this parable, he responded to Peter's question as to whether we should forgive someone up to seven times. Of course, Jesus responded, "I tell you, not seven times, but seventy-seven times" (some manuscripts say seventy times seven). At that time, the Jewish leaders taught that forgiving someone more than three times was unnecessary. Based on this, Peter probably thought that he was being incredibly generous. The point Jesus was making was that our forgiveness should not be limited to a specific number. He was pointing out that there is no limit to our obligation to forgive others. The grace of God has no limit, and forgiveness comes through grace.

Prevention

In Ephesians 4:26-27, Paul calls upon us to forgive others before the sun goes down to not give the devil a foothold. Paul's point was that we shouldn't let our offense continue for an extended period of time in order to prevent sinful consequences. We need to resolve issues as quickly as possible.

When we work to resolve our anger quickly, we prevent Satan from using that anger to create bitterness in our hearts making it more difficult to forgive. When we hold onto our anger, we constantly relive the painful event and build resentment towards others. This anger and resentment makes us feel justified in wanting to further punish the other person.

Summary

Forgiveness is such a foundation to a healthy spiritual relationship with God, that it must become an area in which we focus on ridding ourselves of any unforgiveness. When we harbor unforgiveness in our lives, it will prevent us from experiencing the full love of God and will ultimately result in emotional, spiritual and physically problems in our own health. We need to remember that forgiveness is more for our benefit than for the benefit of those that we forgive.

Bridge of Forgiveness: Study Questions

What is Forgiveness

How would you describe forgiveness?

What are some ways that we have had to forgive each other in the past?

Why is it important to release yourself from the obligation to punish?

Why Forgiveness is Important

What have been the hardest things for you to forgive and why?

Why do you think God wants us to offer the same forgiveness to others that we have received from him?

What impact will recognizing God's perfect judgments increase your emotional, physical and spiritual health?

In what ways do you find it challenging to let God be the judge of the sins committed by others against you?

How are we drawn closer together through acts of forgiveness?

What relationships do you have that may need some mending and what are some actions you could take to help mend the relationship?

What Hinders Forgiveness

What are some of the things done by others that offend you the most?

What expectations do we have of each other and how could they be damaging to our relationship?

What are some of the things we do that tend to prolong our anger?

What are some things we could do to help remove our anger as quickly as possible?

Why do you think pride has such a damaging effect on forgiveness?

When was a time that you were shown forgiveness and how did it make you feel?

Why do you think that people often fail to recognize their sinfulness and spend more time accusing others?

What Promotes Forgiveness

What are some characteristics of a humble spouse?

When is it most difficult for us to demonstrate humility?

What are ways that you try to demonstrate your love for your spouse?

How would you rate the environment of love in your home?

What are some ways that your spouse makes you feel loved?

What are some ways that we show our respect for Christ?

What are some of the ways that Christ showed his love toward mankind?

Do we make it easy for each other to repent and ask forgiveness?

How Forgiveness is Demonstrated by God

In what ways do you find it easy or difficult to accept God's forgiveness of your sins?

Why do you think it is important to offer forgiveness before someone says that they are sorry?

How does it make you feel when someone is eager to show you forgiveness and accept you as you are?

What are some ways you can demonstrate to your spouse the tenderness and acceptance of the father in the parable of the prodigal son?

Why do you think so many people view forgiveness as a difficult thing to offer?

What are some ways that would help you delight in showing mercy and forgiveness?

How Forgiveness is Demonstrated in Marriage

Why was Christ's death on the cross an acceptable atonement for our sins?

In what ways is it difficult to accept that Christ's crucifixion was a sufficient atonement for the actions of those that hurt us?

Do we tend to demonstrate a willingness to forgive or a desire to add to the punishment already provided by the crucifixion?

What are some ways that you could show comfort and support after offering forgiveness?

What are some things that can hinder you from showing comfort and support after offering forgiveness?

What would make it easier for you to forgive when you don't want to forgive?

Why do you think couples tend to escalate their arguments?

How can escalation create an environment that is harder to forgive?

What are some ways to prevent escalation?

Steps to Forgiveness

In what ways do you find it easy or difficult to pray when you are angry at others?

Why do you think God wants to be involved in your process of forgiving others?

What are some positive things you could focus on when you are angry at someone?

Do you find it easy or difficult to comprehend how much God has forgiven you?

Do you tend to hold others to a higher standard than you have held yourself? In what ways?

What are some steps you could take to help each other quickly release your anger?

Chapter 4: The Bridge of Healing

The concept of healing can be a challenging topic for any people as it carries many questions. These questions may involve a lot of pain and they may even challenge many beliefs. Some questions may include:

1. Does God really heal today?
2. How much do we trust God vs. trust doctors?
3. How do I handle healing within my marriage?
4. Is sickness a result of sin?

We are going to discuss what healing is, what hinders it, the responsibility you have as a spouse of someone that needs healing and ways that God demonstrates healing.

What is Healing

Let's start but defining what we mean by healing. There are several aspects to our overall health. Healing is the process of being restored back to our intended state either spiritually, emotionally and/or physically. God also heals us from the inside out. God is often focused on the inside while we are focused on the outside. We live in a world that has been made imperfect by the sinful nature of mankind. As a result, every person will need some type of personal healing during their lifetime. Unfortunately, many people feel that it is necessary to hide their struggles and never seek the healing that they need.

In Mark 2:17 Jesus said, "*It is not the healthy who need a doctor, but the sick. I have not come to call the righteous, but the sinners.*" Romans 3:23 says that "*all have sinned and fallen short of the glory of God.*" Therefore, every one of us is in need of spiritual healing.

In Romans, 5:8 it says that "*God demonstrated his own love for us in this: while we were still sinners, Christ died for us.*" God did not wait for us to become healthy before he healed us. Therefore, if you want to show the love of Christ in your marriage, you should expect to love your spouse through their needs of healing.

Let's take a look at physical, emotional and spiritual healing in more detail. A very significant part of Christ's ministry focused healing. We read in Mark 4:23 that "Jesus went throughout Galilee, teaching in their synagogues, preaching the good news of the Kingdom, and healing every disease and sickness among the people."

Physical Healing

God's desire to provide physical healing to mankind is clearly evident in the miracles of Jesus. When we consider that God desires to draw us close to him in a personal relationship, we begin to see why healing the sick is such an important focus for God. When we experience the grace of healing, it softens our hearts and draws us closer to the Healer. You see this in the woman that suffered from bleeding in Matthew 9:20-22. She did everything she could to just get to Jesus and touch him.

If your spouse sees you as willing to be part of the healing process in their life vs. condemning them for their struggles, then they will draw close to you. We will go into that later in terms of what our role is in the healing process.

Emotional Healing

Emotional healing is often one of the most challenging aspects of a marriage relationship. It is important to understand that while we use the term emotional, it does not mean that there may not be physical causes and aspects to the issue. For emotional healing, we refer to issues that clearly impact our emotions such as depression, anxiety, fear, rage, stress, and hopelessness.

Let's look at three passages to gain a better understanding of emotion struggles within scripture:

> "And now my life seeps away. Depression haunts my days. At night my bones are filled with pain, which gnaws at me relentlessly."
>
> - Job 30:16-17

> "For when we came into Macedonia, this body of ours had no rest, but we were harassed at every turn – conflicts on the outside, fears within. But God, who comforts the downcast, comforted us by the coming of Titus."
>
> - 2 Corinthians 7:5-6

> "They went to a place called Gethsemane, and Jesus said to his disciples, "Sit here while I pray." He took Peter, James and John along with him, and he began to be deeply distressed and troubled."
>
> - Mark 14:32-33

We read in these passages about several instances where worthy men of God and even Christ, struggled emotionally. Emotional struggles and trauma are normal aspects of humanity. They are not indications of personal sin or spiritual weakness, but may be a result of painful experiences in the past or chemical imbalances. For example, in John 9:1-3, the disciples ask Jesus whether a man that was born blind was blind because of his sins or his parent's sins. Jesus replied that it was not because of sin, but so that God could be glorified through him. There can be many reasons why healing is needed.

The passage in Mark 14 about Christ struggling emotionally is really astounding. The Greek words for distressed and troubled are *Ekthambeo*, which means to be terrified and *Ademoneo*, which means to be depressed. Christ went through a period of being terrorized and great depression, yet we know that he did not sin. This should be a quite an assurance for those that struggle emotionally.

Regardless of the cause, the resulting emotional state is not one that God wants us to continue in throughout our life (*Psalm 147:3 – God heals the brokenhearted and bandages their wounds*). However, God may use it as an opportunity to strengthen us prior to healing. We also read in Isaiah 61 that "*He has sent me to bind up the brokenhearted, to proclaim freedom for the captives and release from darkness for the prisoners.*" If we are to emulate the love of Christ, we all have a role to play in healing others, especially our spouse.

Spiritual Healing

There are two aspects of spiritual healing. The first one is found in spiritual separation from God, which was dealt with by Christ's death on the cross. Isaiah 53:5 is prophesy about Christ and says, "*But he was pierced for our transgressions, he was crushed for our iniquities; the punishment that brought us peace was upon him, and by his wounds we are healed.*"

As noted above, healing is the process of being restored back to an intended state. Our sinful nature separates us from God, which was not intended at creation. After salvation, God begins the process of sanctification as he brings us to spiritual completion (Philippians 1:6).

The second aspect of spiritual healing has its roots in Ephesians 6:12 which says, "*For our struggle is not against flesh and blood, but against the rulers, against the authorities, against the powers of this dark world and against the spiritual forces of evil in the heavenly realm.*" Spiritual healing is about overcoming the painful effects of spiritual oppression and the spiritual attacks made against us by Satan. It is important to appreciate that these struggles are varied and real and to understand that the healing process required may be different than in other areas of healing.

Why Healing is Important

Central to the Gospel

Now that we have established a framework around the different aspects of healing, let us consider why healing is so important. We mentioned earlier that healing was a significant aspect of Christ's ministry on earth. When Jesus sent out the twelve disciples in Matthew 10:1, he made it very clear that they make healing a central part of their ministry in preaching the gospel. He did not however heal for the purpose of recognition as he often instructed the healed not to tell anyone. From this, we see a God that views our healing as an important part of the process of salvation. The physical and emotional healing of Christ pointed to the spiritual healing that he wants everyone to receive (Matthew 9:12-13).

Draws us Close to Healer

In Luke 18:35-41, we find the story of Jesus healing the blind beggar. In verse 40, Jesus stopped and ordered the man to be brought to him. This is important as it illustrates that to be healed, we must be drawn closer to the healer. During this time of closeness, we are able to express our inner desires and make ourselves vulnerable with our deepest needs. This is the point when intimacy begins to emerge. When we are willing to participate with God as he heals our spouse (physically, emotionally or spiritually), we will be drawn closer to our spouse in greater intimacy.

Increases our Faith

It takes faith to accept and follow God. The desire to be healed has the ability to increase our faith. This happens at the point when we decide that we want healing so much that we are willing to accept a miracle that only God can provide. This burning desire to be healed brings us to the point that he is able to connect with us at a personal level.

When we look at the men that lowered their paralyzed friend through the roof down to Jesus to be healed in Mark 2:1-5, we also begin to see the role that we play in helping others get close to Christ for healing. It was the faith of the paralyzed man's friends that healed the paralyzed man. Christ may want your faith to heal your spouse. When your spouse struggles, do you offer faith or criticism?

Jesus often talked about healing in the context of faith. It takes faith to accept and follow God. Of course, we also have to battle through the fear of faith. In Luke 8:50, Jesus said to Jairus who wanted his daughter healed (and ultimately raised from the dead), "*Don't be afraid; just believe, and she will be healed.*" The desire to be healed has the ability to increase our faith. This happens at the point when we decide that we want healing so much that we are willing to accept a miracle that only God can provide.

> "*Jesus said to him, 'Receive your sight; your faith has healed you.'*"
>
> - *Luke 18:42*

> "*In Lystra there sat a man who was lame. He had been that way from birth and had never walked. He listened to Paul as he was speaking. Paul looked directly at him, saw that he had faith to be healed and called out, 'Stand up on your feet!' At that, the man jumped up and began to walk.*"
>
> - *Acts 14:8-10*

This burning desire to be healed brings us to the point that he is able to connect with us at a personal level. Faith is important for trust to exist in a relationship. We also need to trust and have faith in our spouse.

What Hinders Healing

It often doesn't take much to hinder healing in our lives. Refusing to visit the doctor over a minor infection can ultimately lead to much more serious consequences in our health. Similarly, failing to properly address needed healing within a marriage relationship can cause petty issues to consolidate and become major obstacles to overcome. This can be further complicated when we actively hinder a healing process.

Harsh Words

Many people struggle throughout their life from harsh words spoken over them, particularly as children. The emotional wounds these words leave are real and painful and often take many years to overcome. Proverbs 15:4 says, "*Gentle words are a tree of life; a deceitful tongue crushes the spirit.*"

It is often easy to speak negative words towards others in the specific areas that they have struggles and need healing. Consider a person that struggles with insecurity and a spouse that criticizes them by saying that they are embarrassed by how quiet their spouse is around friends. This harsh word only serves to reinforce the spouse's insecurity. It is important to recognize that our harsh words will actually prolong the healing process in a needed area.

Hardened Heart

In Matthew 13 the disciples ask Jesus why he talked in parables. In verses 14-15 he responded, "*This fulfills the prophesy of Isaiah that says, 'When you hear what I say, you will not understand, when you see what I do, you will not comprehend, for the hearts of these people are hardened, and their ears cannot hear, and they have closed their eyes so their eyes cannot see, and their ears cannot hear, and their hearts cannot understand, and they cannot turn to me and let me heal them.'*"

A hardened heart occurs when we become spiritually insensitive and lose sight of God. It can result in us not being able to go to the healer and be healed. A hardened heart can happen very easily. It even happened to the disciples right after Christ performed the miracle of feeding 5,000 people with five loaves of bread and two fish (Mark 6:45-52). After the feeding of the 5,000 people, the disciples got in a boat to head across the lake to Bethsaida. During the night while the disciples were still on the boat, Jesus walked across the water and got in the boat and calmed the wind and the waves. It says that the disciples were amazed because they still didn't understand the feeding of the 5,000 people because their hearts were too hard.

When we have a hardened heart, we often fail to recognize God even when he is walking to us. When we don't recognize our healer, it makes it more difficult to be healed.

Lack of Faith

While a desire for healing can increase our faith, a lack of faith can also prevent healing. The difference is often a result of the beliefs and desire of the individual. This becomes particularly important when God wants to use a spouse to help heal their mate. Comments that demonstrate a lack of faith like, "You will never change!" can have a detrimental impact on your spouse and reinforce a feeling of hopelessness.

When they came to the crowd, a man approached Jesus and knelt before him. "Lord, have mercy on my son," he said. "He has seizures and is suffering greatly. He often falls into the fire or into the water. I brought him to your disciples, but they could not heal him". "You unbelieving and perverse generation," Jesus replied, "How long shall I stay with you? How long shall I put up with you? Bring the boy here to me." Jesus rebuked the demon, and it came out of the boy, and he was healed at that moment. Then the disciples came to Jesus in private and asked, "Why couldn't we drive it out?" He replied, "Because you have so little faith. Truly I tell you, if you have faith as small as a mustard seed, you can say to this mountain, 'Move from here to there,' and it will move. Nothing will be

impossible for you."

- *Matthew 17:41-21*

In the above passage we find that the lack of faith by the disciples hindered their ability to heal the boy.

Not Asking

Just like it takes us going to a doctor and asking for the doctor to heal us, we have to go to Christ and ask him to heal us. When we decide to bottle up our struggles inside, we prevent our healing. We have to be open and honest with God about our needs. Healing is sometimes instantaneous, but often a process. In either case, it requires that we ask for it.

As Jesus approached Jericho, a blind man was sitting by the roadside begging. When he heard the crowd going by, he asked what was happening. They told him, "Jesus of Nazareth is passing by." He called out, "Jesus, Son of David, have mercy on me!" Those who led the way rebuked him and told him to be quiet, but he shouted all the more, "Son of David, have mercy on me!" Jesus stopped and ordered the man be brought to him. When he came near, Jesus asked him, "What do you want me to do for you?" "Lord, I want to see," he replied. Jesus said to him, "Receive your sight; your faith has healed you."

- *Luke 18: 35-42*

If the blind man had not called out for help and asked Jesus for healing then he may never have received is sight. At times, we also need to ask louder than those that try to keep us from being healed.

What Promotes Healing

Humility

God continuously reveals himself with a desire to heal his people. However, it is important to recognize that his desire to heal is based on a desire for a healthy relationship. This often requires humility on our part. Humility puts us in a position to accept God for who he is and to take the steps necessary to draw close to him so that he can heal us. In 2 Chronicles 7:14 God spoke and said, "*If my people, who are called by my name, will humble themselves and pray and seek my face and turn from their wicked ways, then I will hear from heaven, and I will forgive their sin and will heal their land.*"

Sincerity

In 2 Kings, there is a story about King Hezekiah. He became seriously ill and went to the Lord in tearful, honest prayer.

In those days Hezekiah became ill and was at the point of death. The prophet Isaiah son of Amoz went to him and said, "This is what the LORD says: Put your house in order, because you are going to die; you will not recover." Hezekiah turned his face to the wall and prayed to the LORD, "Remember, LORD, how I have walked before you faithfully and with wholehearted devotion and have done what is good in your eyes." And Hezekiah wept bitterly. Before Isaiah had left the middle court, the word of the LORD came to him: "Go back and tell Hezekiah, the ruler of my people, 'This is what the LORD, the God of your father David, says: I have heard your prayer and seen your tears; I will heal you.'"

- 2 Kings 20:1-5

God responds to us when we pray and he also recognizes our sincerity. Not only did he hear King Hezekiah's prayer, but he saw his tears. We should never be embarrassed or feel that it demonstrates any weakness in our faith to go to God in tearful prayer to reveal our inner-most desires. Sometimes, this is the exact point that God responds.

After God told King Hezekiah that he would heal him, Isaiah provided some necessary medical treatment (verse 7). It is important to recognize that even after God tells us that he will heal us, he may require the involvement of others (e.g., a doctor, psychologist, therapist, spouse, etc.).

Worship

Worship is the demonstration of our recognition of God for who he really is and our desire to have fellowship with him. It brings us to God. This is God's ultimate desire. Once we draw close to God, he is able heal us. The fear of the Lord is the acknowledgement of who he is which brings us to the point of worship.

Worship the Lord your God, and his blessing will be on your food and water. I will take away sickness from among you.

- Exodus 23:25

Do not be wise in your own eyes; fear the Lord and shun evil. This will bring health to your body and nourishment to your bones.

- Proverbs 3:7

Prayer and Confession

Many people recognize the importance of prayer when they want to ask God for his intervention and healing. However, many people also don't precede that with confession. The reason confession is important is that it breaks down the barriers that emerge between us and God and allows us to drawn close to him, our healer. James 5: 13-16 encourages us to confess or sins with one another and to pray for each other. This is an important role of a spouse within a marriage. We should have the freedom and health in our relationships to confess our struggles. It is also just as important to have the comfort of knowing that our spouse will not condemn you, but instead intercede on your behalf with God.

Is anyone among you in trouble? Let them pray. Is anyone happy? Let them sing songs of praise, Is anyone among you sick? Let them call the elders of the church to pray over them and anoint them with oil in the name of the Lord. And the prayer offered in faith will make the sick person well; the Lord will raise them up. If they have sinned, they will be forgiven. Therefore confess your sins to each other and pray for each other so that you may be healed. The prayer of a righteous person is powerful and effective.

- James 5:13-16

Faith

While it is clear that a lack of faith can hinder healing, it is equally clear that having faith can promote healing. Sometimes we need to exclaim as the disciples did in Luke 17:5, "*Increase our faith!*" Remember that faith is given by God, so we need to earnestly seek him in prayer to strengthen us (Romans 12:31 and Thessalonians 3:10).

Jesus turned and saw her. "Take heart, daughter," he said, "your faith has healed you." And the woman was healed at that moment.

- Matthew 9:22

Then Jesus said to her, "Woman, you have great faith! Your request is granted." And her daughter was healed at that moment.

- Matthew 15:28

"Go," said Jesus, "your faith has healed you." Immediately he received his sight and followed Jesus along the road.

- Mark 10:52

How Healing is Demonstrated by God

With Compassion

God's desire for a relationship with mankind is demonstrated in a powerful way as we see the compassion that he has in healing the sick. The compassion that Christ had for the sick was so strong that it became a central part of his ministry. He saw the sick and wanted to heal them. God does not want us to be sick, whether it is physically, emotionally or spiritually. He wants to bring us to completion as he restores us to our intended state.

God is ready to heal and wants to respond to us. In Psalm 30:2, David writes *"Lord my God, I called to you for help, and you healed me."* Notice that he didn't write that he called to God for help and God rebuked him for all his past inadequacies and gave him an "I told you so" lecture. No, God just responded with compassion.

With Conditions

While God has a strong compassion and desire to heal, he also has a primary goal to bring us into a relationship with him. That relationship requires that we put off the things that hinder us (Hebrews 12:1). Occasionally, God requires certain necessary preconditions be met before he provides healing. That does not mean that any unmet need for healing is a result of something separating us from God, but it is something that should be asked in thoughtful prayer. Remember, whenever God had a precondition for healing in Scripture, he made it well know.

> *He said, "If you listen carefully to the Lord your God and do what is right in his eyes, if you pay attention to his commands and keep all his decrees, I will not bring on you any of the diseases I brought on the Egyptians, for I am the Lord, who heals you."*
>
> *- Exodus 15:26*

They answered, "If you return the ark of the god of Israel, do not send it back to him without a gift; by all means send a guilt offering to him. Then you will be healed, and you will know why his hand has not been lifted from you.

- 1 Samuel 6:3

If my people, who are called by my name, will humble themselves and pray and seek my face and turn from their wicked ways, then I will hear from heaven, and I will forgive their sin and will heal their land.

- 2 Chronicles 7:14

With Purpose

As Christ began his ministry, he immediately set out to heal people. He recognized the need people had for complete healing. Jesus was purposeful in where he went and who he spent time with so that he could accomplish his ministry. He was always under the direction of the Father.

In Matthew 9:11-13, the Pharisees asked the disciples why Jesus ate with tax collectors and sinners. Jesus quickly responded, "*It is not the healthy who need a doctor, but the sick. But go and learn what this means: I desire mercy, not sacrifice. For I have not come to call the righteous, but sinners.*" Jesus knew that he had to be intentional about healing.

Jesus went throughout Galilee, teaching in their synagogues, proclaiming the good news of the kingdom, and healing every disease and sickness among the people. News about him spread all over Syria, and people brought to him all who were ill with various diseases, those suffering severe pain, the demon-possessed, those having seizures, and the paralyzed; and he healed them.

- Matthew 4:23-24

How Healing is Demonstrated in Marriage

Acceptance

As Christians, we are called to accept others with the love of Christ. When others are struggling, it is not our responsibility to pass judgment on them, but instead, show them love and acceptance so that Christ can do a good work in them.

Very truly I tell you, whoever accepts anyone I send accepts me; and whoever accepts me accepts the one who sent me.

- *John 13:20*

Accept one another, then, just as Christ accepted you, in order to bring praise to God.

- *Romans 15:7*

Even more in a marriage relationship, we are called to a special level of caring acceptance in the model of Christ. As we have explored, Christ saw healing as being critically important in our relationship with God. In the same way, we need to accept our spouse where they are and love them through the good times and bad. What great reward there will be for the one that loves their spouse in a way that draws them even closer to Christ!

In this same way, husbands ought to love their wives as their own bodies. He who loves his wife loves himself. After all, no one ever hated their own body, but they feed and care for their body, just as Christ does the church.

- *Ephesians 5:28-29*

Prayer

Prayer is central to the Christian life, particularly as we are called to pray for others. God wants to act through the prayers of mankind. We should make it a daily act to pray for our spouse to bring healing and to keep them in good health.

In Genesis 20:17, we read about Abraham praying to God to heal his wife and others so that they could have children again. We also see this again in Genesis 25:21 where Isaac prayed to the Lord on behalf of his wife because she was childless. After this, God answered Isaac's prayer and Rebekah, his wife, became pregnant.

James 5:16 also says to confess our sins and pray for each other so that we can be healed. Prayer is powerful and should be used with great enthusiasm.

Encouragement

We can have a great impact on others through words of encouragement. Science has shown the helpful effects of a positive attitude in the healing process. Our words of encouragement may be the one thing needed to help our spouse. Proverbs 16:24 says, "*Gracious words are a honeycomb, sweet to the soul and healing to the bones.*" Paul calls us to this in Roman's 1:11-12 when he says, "*I long to see you so that I may impart to you some spiritual gift to make you strong – that is, that you and I may be mutually encouraged by each other's faith.*

The process of healing can often feel like a battle for many people. We should realize the power that encouraging our spouse can have in helping them fight that battle. Throughout battles in the Old Testament, we read about the need to encourage one another:

But the Israelites encouraged one another and again took up their positions where they stationed themselves the first day.

-   Judges 20:22

David told the messenger, "Say this to Joab: 'Don't let this upset you; the sword devours one as well as another. Press the attack against the city and destroy it.' Say this to encourage Joab."

- 2 Samuel 11:25

But commission Joshua, and encourage and strengthen him, for he will lead this people across and will cause them to inherit the land that you will see.

- Deuteronomy 3:28

Steps to Healing

Patience

God's timing and purpose is often a mystery. We are however not called to understand that mystery, but to pray continuously and to wait patiently. This is not always easy, but when we place our confidence in the Lord and endure hardship, we know that he will welcome us as a good and faithful servant. There is a time for healing to take place (Ecclesiastes 3:3) and we need to be patient for that time to arrive. As it is said in Psalm 27:14, we need to wait for the Lord, be strong and take heart and wait for the Lord.

I say to myself, "The Lord is my portion; therefore I will wait for him."

- Lamentations 3:24

Attitude

We can choose our attitude. Our attitude whether good or bad will impact our healing process. We need to also be mindful of how we are impacting our spouse's attitude and ensure that we are being responsible with our words.

Proverbs says that a happy heart makes the face cheerful, but heartache crushes the spirit (15:13) and that the human spirit can endure in sickness, but a crushed spirit who can bear? (18:14).

Prayer and Anointing

The process of prayer and anointing with oil is often overlooked by couples as a step in the healing process. Anointing with oil is seen throughout scripture as a process of setting apart in dedication to the Lord. It can become a great moment of spiritual intimacy bringing a couple closer together in difficult times.

Is anyone among you sick? Let them call the elders of the church to pray over them and anoint them with oil in the name of the Lord. And the prayer offered in faith will make the sick person well; the Lord will raise them up. If they sinned, they will be forgiven.

- James 5:14-15

They drove out many demons and anointed many sick people with oil and healed them.

- Mark 6:13

Action

Healing sometimes requires action on our part or by others, whether it is through the prompting of the Holy Spirit, or words from a pastor, doctor, spouse, etc. We should be mindful of what we should do to aid our own personal healing process, as well as, ways we can help our spouse. Some people don't want healing. For others, it takes time to let go of past hurts that will enable healing.

In John 9:6-7, Jesus put mud on a blind man's eyes; however, the man wasn't healed at that point. Instead, Jesus told the man to go wash in the Pool of Siloam. It wasn't until the man took action to wash himself that he was healed and could see. We also saw action on the part of the men that lowered the paralyzed man through the roof for Jesus to heal him (Mark 2:3-5). Waiting idly by hoping for healing is often not enough. It requires us to do something drastic and take action.

There are times that we may not understand what God calls us to do before we are healed. Like in the case of Naaman in 2 Kings 5:1-15, it may require humility. Previously, we discussed the importance of humility to promote healing. For humility to be effective, it requires action on our part to demonstrate that humility. Crying out for help often requires great humility, but may be the first necessary step towards healing.

Summary

Everyone needs to have some level of healing in their lives. Being an instrument of God in our spouse's life is one of the greatest gifts that God can give you. It will create a lasting intimacy in your marriage that will allow your relationship to grow to new levels. However, healing requires significant patience, which leads us to the next bridge.

Bridge of Healing: Study Questions

What is Healing

What types of healing have you experienced during your lifetime?

What types of healing do you think you still need?

Describe a time that you went through a physical hardship and what were the challenges you experienced?

What were the causes of depression for Job, Christ and Paul and how were they handled?

In what ways have your struggled emotionally and what do you think were the causes?

Do you believe that spiritual oppression is still prevalent today?

How would you describe the process of your salvation and sanctification thus far in life?

Why Healing is Important

Why do you think Jesus started the commissioning of the twelve disciples by giving them the authority to heal?

What are some things that your spouse does that make it easier for you to handle difficult times?

Why do you think healing has the effect of drawing us close to the healer?

Why do you think God uses healing as a way of drawing us close to him?

Describe how you have experienced God during your life?

How would you rate your level of faith any why?

What Hinders Healing

In what ways have you been criticized in the past?

Why do you think words are so powerful?

In what ways can you become spiritually insensitive and lose sight of God?

What are some ways that you can focus on drawing close to God with a softened heart?

Why do you think God desires to use us in the process of healing others?

What are some ways that you can be more supportive of the needs of your spouse?

Do you find it easy or difficult to ask God for a miracle and why?

What Promotes Healing

How do we demonstrate our humility with God and with each other?

What makes a request sincere?

What are some ways that you can make your spouse comfortable being sincere with you?

What are some ways that we can worship God together?

In what ways can a couple make it safe to confess their struggles with one another?

What are some ways that you can make your relationship safer to be honest with one another?

In what areas do you think you could improve your faith?

How Healing is Demonstrated by God

Do you find it difficult to respond to the healing needs of others with compassion? Why?

In what ways have you demonstrated compassion towards each other in your struggles?

What do the preconditions God set forth in the following passages have in common? Exodus 15:26, 1 Samuel 6:3 and 2 Chronicles 7:14

How would you describe the purpose in Christ's ministry?

How does God's purpose as it pertains to healing impact your view of your role as a spouse?

How Healing is Demonstrated in Marriage

What are some ways that one can communicate that they don't accept their spouse for who they are?

What are some ways that one can communicate that they do accept their spouse for who they are?

Why do you think demonstrating our acceptance of our spouse can have such a dramatic impact on their healing?

How would you rate your prayer time for each other?

What are some ideas to improve your prayer time for each other?

What are some ways you can encourage your spouse?

Steps to Healing

How would you rate your patience individually and as a couple?

What are some ways you could increase your patience?

What are some ways that your spouse is able to positively impact your attitude?

What are times in your relationship when anointing with oil should be considered?

Why do you think it is hard for some people to do what is necessary for healing?

Why do you think it was difficult for Naama to cleanse himself in the Jordan in 2 Kings 5:1-15?

Are there any steps you feel you should take in your life as you continue to improve your physical, emotional or spiritual health?

Chapter 5: The Bridge of Patience

Patience is something we all need, but it may not be a fun process to develop it. The need for patience has been a common theme throughout history. Here are just a few quotes during different time periods:

It is easier to find men who will volunteer to die, than to find those who are willing to endure pain with patience. – Julius Caesar

How poor are they that have not patience! What wound did ever heal but by degrees? – William Shakespeare

Genius is eternal patience. – Michelangelo

Patience and diligence, like faith, remove mountains. – William Penn

Patience and perseverance have a magical effect before which difficulties disappear and obstacles vanish. – John Quincy Adams

I'm extraordinarily patient provided I get my own way in the end. – Margaret Thatcher

Margaret Thatcher probably speaks for most of us in how we approach patience. It is clear that patience is a challenge for many, if not all of us. Yet, we know that patience is a fruit of the Spirit. If it is a fruit of the Spirit, then it can be developed in our life. But first, we need to understand what patience really means. We like to view patience the following ways:

1. A fruit of the Spirit
2. Longsuffering
3. A reflection of love
4. Forbearance

5. Constancy

What is Patience

<u>Fruit of the Spirit</u>
Galatians 5:22 says that patience is a fruit of the Spirit. The fruit of the Spirit represents the qualities that are produced by the Holy Spirit. When we accept Christ, the Holy Spirit lives in and works through us to produce the fruit found in Galatians 5:22. Just like an apple tree, the Holy Spirit cannot help but produce its fruit. The fruit is always ready to bloom. How much fruit is produced depends on you. A good farmer does not leave his crops alone to see if they will produce fruit, but instead fertilizes, cultivates, and protects his crop to yield the greatest fruit.

It is important to recognize that patience is a fruit of the Spirit and not a personality trait. If we view it as a personality trait, then it suggests that it is part of our genetic make-up. We either have it or we don't. When we see it as a fruit of the Spirit, we know that it is available to everyone.

<u>Longsuffering</u>
1 Thessalonians 5:14 says, "*We urge you, brothers, warn those who are idle, encourage the timid, help the weak, be patient with everyone.*" Sometimes it is difficult to be patient with anyone, yet we are called to be patient with everyone. The Greek word for patient in this verse is *makrothumeo*, which means longsuffering. *Makrothumeo* comes from two words meaning long and temper. It is the opposite of a short-temper in that is does not over-react in anger. It also has a connotation of showing bravery in handling difficult situations. It recognizes that showing this type of patience is not easy, but takes courage in restraining yourself as you go through difficulties.

Reflection of Love

Patience is also a reflection of love. 1 Corinthians 13 is a well know passage describing love. The very first word to describe agape (unconditional) love is patient. It is the same Greek word, *makrothumeo*, found in 1 Thessalonians 5:14, which means longsuffering. If love is patient, then when we show patience, we are showing love. Also, if unconditional love is patient, then our patience should also be unconditional. Think about that.

Forbearance

Have you ever had a bad day and responded harshly to your spouse even though you didn't mean it? Have you said words that you wish you could have stopped before they left your mouth? We all have experienced those moments of regret. We have all also been on the receiving end of those moments of regret. How do you respond when you are the one receiving those harsh words?

2 Timothy 2:24 says, "*The Lord's bond-servant must not be quarrelsome, but be kind to all, able to teach, patient when wronged.*" The Greek word for patience in this verse is *anexikakos*, which means forbearing. Forbearing is similar to longsuffering. It reveals a willingness to give others the benefit of the doubt and keep your temper under control in response to an evil act. In other words, you are not easily provoked and have self-control in responding to others.

Constancy

1 Timothy 1:15-16 says, "*Here is a trustworthy saying that deserves full acceptance: Christ Jesus came into the world to save sinners—of whom I am the worst. But for that very reason I was shown mercy so that in me, the worst of sinners, Christ Jesus might display his unlimited patience as an example for those who would believe on him and receive eternal life.*"

Paul describes himself as the worst of sinners, based on how he used to persecute Christians. He says this not to demean himself, but instead to describe the extent of Christ's patience with us. Christ is willing to wait patiently for us to come to him, even while we are at our worst. The Greek word for patience in this verse is *makrothumia*, which means a constant endurance and steadfastness. It reflects a patience that does not change but perseveres through difficult times. It is a patience that can be counted upon.

Why Patience is Important

There are four main reasons why we see patience as so important to a relationship: Handling Conflict, Provides Hope, Turns God to Us and Creates Thankfulness.

Handling Conflict
Proverbs 25:15 says, "*Through patience a ruler can be persuaded, and a gentle tongue can break a bone.*"

In handling conflict, there is a funny story about a child that is told to sit down at the dinner table. In a reluctant response, the child says, "I will sit down, but in my heart I am still standing." Forcing others into compliance without winning their heart does not end the conflict, it just changes the strategy. Patience is important in conflict as it can allow time for others to come into agreement with us, and also allow time for us to realize that we are wrong.

Provides Hope
Hope is a powerful force. Napoleon Bonaparte once said that "Courage is like love, it must have hope for nourishment." Romans 5:3-5 says, "*Not only so, but we also rejoice in our sufferings, because we know that suffering produces perseverance; perseverance, character; and character, hope. And hope does not disappoint us, because God has poured out his love into our hearts by the Holy Spirit, whom he has given us.*"

The existence of hope allows us to focus on what something could be and not just what it is. In these verses, the Greek word for perseverance is *humpomone*, which also means patience. Hope begins with patience in the midst of difficult times. When you are going through difficult times and want to have hope, remember to focus first on patience. But don't forget that before hope comes, you may need to work on your character.

Turns God to Us
We mentioned earlier that patience turns God to us. Psalm 40:1 says, "I waited patiently for the Lord; he turned to me and heard my cry."

What is waiting patiently? First, it is an attitude. We can wait for something and demonstrate many different attitudes. We can wait with anger, annoyance, contempt, impatience, joy, or peace to name a few. But what is it about patience that allows God to turn to us? The Hebrew word for patience in this verse is *qavah*, which describes an attitude of eagerness and expectation as you wait. It demonstrates that you have faith in God and trust his timing. Think of it as a child waiting for Christmas morning. The child goes to sleep with an inner excitement built upon the belief of what awaits them in the morning.

Thankfulness
Patience also creates thankfulness. In many respects, this may be one of the most powerful results of patience. 1 Thessalonians 1:2-3 says, "*We give thanks to God always for all of you, making mention of you in our prayers; constantly bearing in mind your work of faith and labor of love and steadfastness of hope in our Lord Jesus Christ in the presence of our God and Father.*"

When we are patient with others, it creates thankfulness in the relationship. Thankfulness is a critical component in building intimacy and drawing close to your spouse. When we are thankful for our spouse, it makes us want to become a better spouse and show them our appreciation. This alone can do wonders for a marriage.

What Hinders Patience

Pride

Pride has a way of hindering many fruitful things in our lives. When we focus on our own desires, we begin the process of neglecting the needs of others. We begin to think that our desires are the most important. This leaves little room for patience when we want our own needs satisfied. This also often leads to actions of instant gratification. Ecclesiastes 7:8 says, "*The end of a matter is better than its beginning, and patience is better than pride.*"

Weariness

When we become burned out, it is difficult to be patient and endure hardship. In Matthew 11:28, Christ makes the offer to those that are tired and burdened with the trials of life. He says that he will give rest (enduring patience). What is making you weary in life? Is your job tiring you out to the point that you come home and have no patience with the kids? Think about the simple impact that a lack of sleep can have on your patience.

Sin

Hebrews 12:1 says, "*Therefore, since we are surrounded by such a great cloud of witnesses, let us throw off everything that hinders and the sin that so easily entangles. And let us run with enduring patience the race marked out for us.*" Before we run the race set before us with enduring patience (Greek, *hupomone*), we must get rid of the sin that entangles us. When we are entangled, it preoccupies our mind with the sin and does not allow us to focus on where God is leading us. When we lose our focus, we allow doubt and other distractions to slow us down and frustrate our endurance.

Lack of Self-Control

Our degree of patience is contingent on our degree of self-control. In other words, if you need more patience, then you need to focus on self-control.

Patience is also needed in order to grow in our spiritual maturity and ability to demonstrate love to others.

In view of all this, make every effort to respond to God's promises. Supplement your faith with a generous provision of more excellence, and more excellence with knowledge, and knowledge with self-control, and self-control with patient endurance, and patient endurance with godliness, and godliness with brotherly affection, and brotherly affection with love for everyone.

- *2 Peter 1:5-7*

What Promotes Patience

Wisdom
Proverbs 19:11 says, "*a person's wisdom yield's patience; it is to one's glory to overlook an offense.*" Some versions of the Bible, translate "patience" in this verse as being slow to anger, as well other similar translations. The concept is similar to being forbearing or longsuffering. Wisdom allows us to interpret situations beyond the moment, which gives us the patience to handle immediately stressful circumstances.

Wisdom is something that is provided by God (Psalm 51:6, Proverbs 2:6). The fear of God is the first step to receiving wisdom (Proverbs 15:33).

Power of God
Colossians 1:11 says, "*being strengthened with all power according to his glorious might so that you may have great endurance and patience.*"

This is great news! When we don't feel like we have the patience to handle a situation, we do not have to become discouraged. God provides us with the patience we need through his strength. Make patience a regular request in your times of prayer. It is best to obtain patience before we need to demonstrate it.
Suffering

When we go through difficult situations, we begin to recognize our inner-strength. This is reflected in Romans 5:3 where it says that suffering produces perseverance. We know our personal limitations and the points that we need the strength provided by the encouragement of others and by the power of God. By working through these situations, we gain an insight into ourselves that we never had before. It gives us the ability to view future situations from a different perspective. A perspective that says, "I can overcome this!"

Comforting Words
Our lack of patience is often a result of fear in our lives. It is the unknown that often scares us and causes us to react in haste. The comforting words and actions by those closest to us, can give us the peace needed to patiently endure the unknown. When your spouse is not patient with you, ask yourself whether they may be fearful of something. If so, responding with comforting words instead of words of frustration may bring about the patience you desire.

For just as we share abundantly in the sufferings of Christ, so also our comfort abounds through Christ. If we are distressed, it is for your comfort and salvation; if we are comforted, it is for your comfort, which produces in you patient endurance of the same sufferings we suffer. And our hope for you is firm, because we know that just as you share in our sufferings, so also you share in our comfort.

- 2 Corinthians 1:5-7

How Patience is Demonstrated by God

Mercy
In 1 Timothy 1:16, Paul tells Timothy about how God demonstrated his patience with Paul during a period that he was doing everything possible to destroy the Christian faith. It was God's mercy that allowed him to wait patiently for the right time to approach Paul and transform his life. Mercy is often described as not giving us what we do deserve. Not only did God not give Paul what he deserved,

but instead gave him the opportunity to come along side him as he transformed history.

Salvation

In 2 Peter 3:15, Peter calls us to regard God's patience with us as salvation. In other words, his patience with us is such an integral part of our salvation that we cannot separate the two. This stresses the importance of patience in a relationship. It is a cornerstone in any reconciliation process.

Individually

God is not just patient. He is specifically patient with each individual person. He sees the value in each person and the importance of being patient with each one. Just as God choose to be patient with you, you need to choose to be patient with your spouse.

The Lord is not slow in keeping his promise, as some understand slowness. Instead he is patient with you, not wanting anyone to perish, but everyone to come to repentance.

- *2 Peter 3:9*

How Patience is Demonstrated in Marriage

Slow to Anger

It is very easy to let our natural instincts take over in the heat of a disagreement. Many people have experienced those times that your anger seemed to appear out of nowhere. In our patience, we need to learn to demonstrate forbearance in those times of disagreement and wait before we speak, just as God is slow to anger, abounding in love and faithfulness (Proverbs 86:15)

Understanding

Proverbs 14:29 says that "*Whoever is patient has great understanding, but one who is quick-tempered displays folly.*"

Taking time to understand each other is a principle that many couples fail to focus on in their marriage. They are too preoccupied with getting their point across or meeting their needs that they don't take time to truly understand their spouse. This is a matter of patience. It starts with us deciding that it is more important to focus first on understanding regardless of the outcome. Understanding is less about what you think you know and more about what your spouse thinks you know. In other words, your focus should be to make sure your spouse believes that you understand them.

Stop the Fight

One of the primary reasons that couples find it difficult to resolve conflict is escalation. Escalation is the process of increasing the intensity (verbally and physically) during a disagreement. Once couples escalate an argument, it is often difficult to find any immediate resolution. It often results in seeds of bitterness being sowed in the relationship. Healthy relationships learn how to control their emotions through patience, and not allow an argument to escalate. Proverbs 15:18 says, "*A hot-tempered person stirs up conflict, but the one who is patient calms a quarrel.*"

Listening

In Acts 26:3, Paul asks the reader to listen to him patiently. What is patient listening? It is the process of letting your spouse speak their mind without interrupting them and not thinking about how you are going to respond before they are done talking. Once you hear what your spouse says, let them know what you heard them say just to be sure there are no miscommunications. Think about how the following responses can yield a very different result in an argument. Response 1: "Am I correct in that you are feeling _____, and when I do _____, it makes you think _____." Response 2: "Why would you think _____. That is the most ridiculous thing I have ever heard." Which response do you think will lead to mutual reconciliation?

Steps to Patience

Decision

Colossians 3:12 says that we are to clothe ourselves with patience. When you clothe yourself, it is an active decision of putting on something. Being patient is a decision. It is not a natural response. Just like any fruit of the Spirit, we can embrace it or reject it.

Role Models

Every couple should seek to have a couple to mentor them. Having a mentor is not a sign of problems or weakness in a marriage, but is a sign of how important a couple views their marriage. No couple has crossed every challenge they will someday face, nor know the outcome of all their decisions. However, other couples have crossed those bridges and can help you view those situations with patience as they guide you in wisdom.

We do not want you to become lazy, but to imitate those who through faith and patience inherit what has been promised.

- Hebrews 6:12

You, however, know all about my teaching, my way of life, my purpose, faith patience, love and endurance.

- 2 Timothy 3:10

Ask God

God is our source to receive all the fruits of the Spirit. He will provide you with the patience and endurance to overcome any circumstance (Romans 15:5). Seek patience and he will also provide greater unity in your relationship.

Summary

One of the strongest verses in scripture about patience is Peter's call that we should regard patience as salvation (2 Peter 3:15). It is such an integral part of the Christian faith. It is a fruit of the Spirit (Gal 5:22) and part of the definition of love (1 Cor. 13). If you demonstrate patience with your spouse, you will build an atmosphere of thankfulness and unity that will allow you to experience a love that is only possible through Christ.

Bridge of Patience: Study Questions

What is Patience

Why do you think it is important to understand that patience is a fruit of the Spirit and not just a personality trait?

When is it hardest for you to show patience?

What difficulties would you make it hard for you to show patience?

Why do you think it is important to demonstrate longsuffering in a marriage?

How do you feel when your spouse is patient with you?

How do you tend to respond when provoked?

How would forbearance help in the midst of a conflict?

How does it feel when you know that you can count on someone to be there for you?

Why Patience is Important

How do you typically respond to others that disagree with you?

What are some ways you could show patience with your spouse during conflict?

What are some things you hope for in your marriage?

What are some of the positive character traits in your spouse?

What are some ways that waiting patiently for your spouse might turn them to you?

What are some ways you could show your thankfulness for each other?

What Hinders Patience

What desires do you have that make you impatient?

What impact do these desires have on how you approach your decisions?

What are some areas where we are weary and can ask Christ for enduring patience?

When do you feel like you have the least amount of patience?

What do you think makes it difficult for you to keep your focus with enduring patience?

Where do you struggle most with self-control?

What Promotes Patience

Why do you think wisdom is helpful in showing patience?

What are some current situations where you would like more wisdom?

What are some ways that you would like to see the power of God work in your life?

What painful experiences have you overcome in the past?

What circumstances would scare you the most? How would you handle it?

How do you typically respond to each other in stressful situations?

What are some ways you could comfort your spouse?

How Patience is Demonstrated by God

How have you been shown mercy in the past?

What are some ways you can show mercy to your spouse?

Why do you think God's patience is an important part of being reconciled to him through our salvation?

In what ways has God been patient with you?

How Patience is Demonstrated in Marriage

What circumstances or things said tend to cause us to become angry the easiest?

What helps you to keep from getting angry?

How do you communicate that you understand your spouse?

Do we tend to escalate arguments? If so, what usually triggers the escalation?

What helps you "cool down" during periods of intense disagreements?

Do you find it difficult to listen patiently? Why?

Steps to Patience

What do you think makes people choose not to demonstrate patience?

What qualities do you think are important for a mentor couple to have?

What are some specific areas where you can ask God for patience?

Chapter 6: The Bridge of Fellowship

What is Fellowship

Fellowship is a key to any successful relationship. There are two primary concepts to understanding fellowship: Unity and Intimate Knowledge.

Unity

Let's start with unity. Since the beginning, God has shown that fellowship is one of the most important attributes of a healthy relationship between God and man. Fellowship is at the core of what enables a relationship to grow and develop. When we look at the creation in Genesis, God appears to act somewhat independently as He creates the heaven and the earth, separates light from darkness, and creates plants and animals. His commands are singular in that He directs the creation and it happens. Such as "Let there be light..." in Genesis 1:3.

However, when He then created man, he made a particular change in His commands as He turned toward fellowship. In Genesis 1:26, He says "Let *us* make man in our image, in our likeness...." The complexity of the relationship between God and man resulted in a unique effort that required the Trinity to focus on working together to create man. Not only was it a team effort, but it was a recognition that man was to reflect the combined image of the Trinity. That is, man was actually a representation of fellowship itself; the image of the Trinity.

"For this reason a man will leave his father and mother and be united to his wife, and they will become one flesh."

- Genesis 2:24

While this passage has often been quoted as a guideline for proper boundaries as a newly married couple leaves their parents and join together to start a new family, it also further explains God's desire for marriage to be a natural reflection of the fellowship of the Trinity on earth. In other words, it is a representation of

God. The word "one" in the above passage is the same Hebrew word (*echad*) that describes God as being "one." See Deuteronomy 6:4 and John 17:7. John 1:1-2 further expands on the notion that not only was there oneness found in the Trinity, but that the Word was <u>with</u> God, suggesting a level of fellowship. In marriage, the physical coming together as one in sexual relations and creating a child that is the combination of both individuals is the final ultimate reflection of the individuality of each person, yet the absolute oneness that results.

Intimate Knowledge

The other aspect of fellowship is intimate knowledge. We are going to look at 2 key passages:

"If you really knew me, you would know my Father as well. From now on, you do know him and have seen him." Philip said, "Lord, show us the Father and that will be enough for us." Jesus answered: "Don't you know me, Philip, even after I have been among you such a long time? Anyone who has seen me has seen the Father. How can you say, 'Show us the Father'? Don't you believe that I am in the Father, and that the Father is in me? The words I say to you are not just my own. Rather, it is the Father, living in me, who is doing his work. Believe me when I say that I am in the Father and the Father is in me; or at least believe on the evidence of the miracles themselves."

- John 14:7-11

"I am the true vine, and my Father is the gardener. He cuts off every branch in me that bears no fruit, while every branch that does bear fruit he prunes so that it will be even more fruitful. You are already clean because of the word I have spoken to you. Remain in me, and I will remain in you. No branch can bear fruit by itself; it must remain in the vine. Neither can you bear fruit unless you remain in me. "I am the vine; you are the branches. If a man remains in me and I in him, he will bear much fruit; apart from me you can do nothing. If anyone does not remain in me, he is like a branch that is thrown away and withers; such branches are picked up, thrown into the fire and burned. If you remain in me and

my words remain in you, ask whatever you wish, and it will be given you. This is to my Father's glory, that you bear much fruit, showing yourselves to be my disciples."

- *John 15:1-8*

Jesus made the above comments during the Last Supper. The Last Supper was a great representation of the fellowship that God desires with us. It was a time of honesty, openness, intimacy, service, encouragement and prayer to mention a few. An interesting comment that Jesus made to Philip was that it is possible to spend regular time with someone and still not know them. Knowing someone requires that you want to truly know them. The kind of fellowship that God desires with us enables us to fully know him.

True fellowship with God enables us to grow stronger spiritually and results in our having a greater impact on the world. As you pursue a closer fellowship with your spouse, you will similarly experience a stronger marriage that will have a greater impact in your life, your children, your family, your friends, and in the world.

Why Fellowship is Important

First, fellowship allows us to work together in teamwork. It also provides us with the opportunity to rejoice in the relationship.

Teamwork
Genesis 2:18 says, "*The Lord God said, "It is not good for the man to be alone. I will make a helper suitable for him."*

This passage gives a unique insight into the relationship of the Trinity and its desire for fellowship. God immediately recognized that it was not good for man to be alone. While man was created in the image of the Trinity, man was an individual and needed an equal to join in fellowship for a complete representation of the Trinity. There is a basic desire for fellowship that is inherent in the way God made us. As the components of the Trinity work together, mankind also has a need to fellowship with a mate to accomplish the work that God desires. Having fellowship with your spouse enables you to become a more complete representation of God's original intent.

Rejoice

Not only does God want us to devote time in fellowship, but He wants us to rejoice in that fellowship. Enjoying each other and rejoicing together is a critical part of fellowship. In many ways, this is the friendship aspect of your relationship. John Gottman, a renowned relationship expert, says that friendship is the heart of a happy marriage and says that friendship fuels the flames of romance (Seven Principles for Making Marriage Work, Crown Publishers, Inc, New York).

"Sacrifice fellowship offerings there, eating them and rejoicing in the presence of the Lord your God."

- Deuteronomy 27:7

A fellowship offering was a type of offering that gave thanks to God in a way that God could rejoice and share in fellowship with mankind. Part of this offering included having a meal. God clearly saw the importance of just taking time to have a meal together and rejoicing over the blessings that God has given you. Christ's death on the cross set us free from the necessity of the various offerings to God as a means of restoring our fellowship with him. However, the purpose behind the offerings provides us with guidance that God saw as a very important aspect of His relationship with His people.

What Hinders Fellowship

<u>Competition</u>

One of the challenges in marriage is that while God designed it to be a reflection of the oneness of the Trinity, He also gave man and woman their own ability to choose to act independently and to choose to act in a healthy dependence with each other. The freewill that God gave mankind not only gives us the ability to choose to have fellowship with Him, but it also gives us the ability to choose to have fellowship with our spouse in a manner that is reflective of God's original design. This is where many married couples find themselves at odds with each other. They do not choose fellowship with their spouse

When God gave Moses the 10 Commandments in Exodus 20, He was not only establishing the Law that defined right and wrong, but He also recognized the importance of maintaining fellowship at a personal level with His people and provided guidance for ways to avoid falling out of fellowship. This was such an important part of the 10 Commandments that the first two commandments focus specifically on this.

You shall have no other gods before me.

- *Exodus 20:3*

You shall not make for yourself an image in the form of anything in heaven above or on earth beneath or in the waters below.

- *Exodus 20:4*

The practical application of this into marriage is far reaching and provides a cornerstone upon which all fellowship with your spouse is built. God made it clear that we should have no other gods or idols before Him. The intimate fellowship that God desires recognizes that when we put competing interests in our lives, it will diminish our fellowship with Him and make it that much harder to follow the remaining commandments.

<u>Words</u>

The third commandment focuses on misusing God's name.

You shall not misuse the name of the Lord your God, for the Lord will not hold anyone guiltless who misuses his name.

- Exodus 20:7

Essentially, this boils down to respect. Showing the proper respect toward your spouse is essential in maintaining an environment where fellowship can be experienced. How often has a careless word spoken toward your spouse ruined what could have been a fine evening together. God recognized that when negative or disrespectful words are spoken, it creates a division in the relationship.

<u>Selfishness</u>

Selfishness is one of the greatest causes of conflict. When selfishness is demonstrated in marriage, it tears apart the core of the "oneness" that God designed in the marriage relationship for the purpose of individual gain.

For where you have envy and selfish ambition, there you find disorder and every evil practice.

- James 3:16

What causes fights and quarrels among you? Don't they come from your desires that battle within you? You desire but do not have, so you kill. You covet but you cannot get what you want, so you quarrel and fight. You do not have because you do not ask God. When you ask, you do not receive, because you ask with wrong motives, that you may spend what you get on your pleasures.

- James 4:1-3

<u>People</u>

In Mark 10:13-15, we see Jesus desiring fellowship with children, which were being hindered from coming to him. The children were being verbally hindered by his disciples. Many couples allow people that are close to them (family and friends) to hinder fellowship with their spouse. Couples need to be careful to not allow those close to them to speak negative words about their spouse, which hinders fellowship. Some couples discuss intimate issues about their marriage relationship with family and friends, which are not objective and qualified to guide them through the issues. Couples should be very mindful to seek guidance from those that are unbiased and trained to provide the guidance sought, which may be a pastor, counselor, or mentor.

What Promotes Fellowship

<u>Transparency</u>

Fellowship requires that we are "living in the light." Living in the light requires that we are transparent and honest. Not only does transparency and honesty keep you in fellowship, but it also draws you into fellowship.

This is the message we have heard from him and declare to you: God is light; in him there is no darkness at all. If we claim to have fellowship with him and yet walk in the darkness, we lie and do not live out the truth. But if we walk in the light, as he is in the light, we have fellowship with one another, and the blood of Jesus, his Son, purifies us from all sin. If we claim to be without sin, we deceive ourselves and the truth is not in us. If we confess our sins, he is faithful and just and will forgive us our sins and purify us from all unrighteousness. If we claim we have not sinned, we make him out to be a liar and his word is not in us.

- 1 John 1:5-10

<u>Quality Time</u>

The fourth commandment focuses on our fellowship with God by honoring the Sabbath. As in any relationship, God recognized how important it is to set aside specific time for each other and to honor each other during this time. God also acknowledges that we are busy and have a lot to get done, so He allows us plenty of time to focus on our tasks. In other words, while he desires that intimate time of weekly fellowship, He doesn't place unreasonable demands on our time, thus supporting the 6 days of labor. This enables us to minimize any distractions during the time of devoted fellowship.

<u>Repentance and Forgiveness</u>

Fellowship between mankind and God is established at the point of forgiveness. It is at that point that He sends the gift of the Holy Spirit resulting in the new creation (2 Corinthians 5:17). While God made forgiveness available to all mankind at the cross, it must be accepted through repentance. This establishes two very important principles for marriage. When couples demonstrate a willingness to repent and forgive, they will experience a greater level of fellowship. Forgiveness is so important to fellowship that it alone is one of The Seven Bridges.

In Acts 2:38-39 says that Peter called for people to repent and be baptized for the forgiveness of sins and then they would receive the Holy Spirit. It was at the point of forgiveness that God joins in fellowship with us through the Holy Spirit.

How Fellowship is Demonstrated by God

Having the kind of fellowship with your spouse that God desires is more complex than talking over breakfast in the morning, watching a movie together or riding bikes on a Saturday afternoon. While these may be very important acts of fellowship, they do not in and of themselves define the level of fellowship that God designed for marriage. To better understand the fullness of fellowship that

God desires to be present in marriage, we are going to take a look at the attributes of fellowship demonstrated by God.

Pursuit

Scripture is clear that God is calling us into fellowship (1 Corinthians 1:9). He is proactive in seeking fellowship with us. Being intentional about fellowship is important in any relationship. When you proactively seek fellowship, you make your spouse feel pursued. This feeling of being pursued was likely a very significant part of the dating experience with your spouse. We are drawn towards those that demonstrate a desire to be with us.

Covenant

God's promises are bound in a covenant (Genesis 9:11-13 and 17:7-11). When one offers a covenant, there is recognition that it will not be rescinded. A covenant also contains a sign as a physical reminder of the covenant. A covenant is important in establishing fellowship, because it provides the comfort and security necessary to fully devote to each other without fear of rejection. 1 John 4:13 states that *"perfect love drives out fear."* God's covenants reflect His perfect love, unconditional love. We do not have to fear separation from God because of the perfect love reflected in his covenants.

A biblical marriage requires that each person make a covenant with their spouse. Through your vows, a covenant of life-long commitment is established, which is physically represented by your wedding rings.

Protection

In Psalm 23, David gives us an insight in the nature of the fellowship of God. David's fellowship with God was a result of God demonstrating a proactive involvement in his life. It was an involvement that reflected both a guide and a defender. The comfort this provided David enabled him to walk boldly into difficult times because he knew God was with him and God was prepared to protect him. David proclaimed that he would dwell with God in fellowship because of the confidence provided through God's protection.

How Fellowship is Demonstrated in Marriage

Activities

Spending time together enjoying activities is vitally important for a couple to experience healthy fellowship. Many couples over-commit themselves with too many obligations that detract them from spending quality time together, or they just don't make time together a priority. Finding areas of common interest are important for couples in experiencing fellowship. It is also important to set aside regular time to spend time together individually, whether that is on a date night, a weekend getaway or going for a walk. These intentional times demonstrate that fellowship with each other is important and a priority in the marriage.

Sex

The description of God bringing Eve to Adam in the garden in Genesis 2:24-25 is a beautiful illustration of fellowship itself in how God brings a husband and wife together and the intimacy that develops in that relationship. Sex is a very important aspect of fellowship. So much so that Paul encourages husbands and wives to not deprive each other, which results in a temptation that destroys fellowship (1 Corinthians 7:5).

Communication

Communication at an intimate level develops fellowship and is essential for a healthy and growing relationship. While many couples appreciate the importance of learning "how" to communicate more effectively, they should also recognize the importance of "what" and "how often" they are communicating. Getting to know your spouse doesn't stop once you say, "I do." When you take the time to continually learn about your spouse's dreams, experiences, fears, anxieties, hopes, struggles, passions and goals, you will find that your relationship with your spouse will grow and strengthen.

We encourage couples to try using the Couch Time! questions at the back of this book to help them develop a regular habit of communication at an intimate level. These questions can used on date nights to guide you into more intimate discussions and away from the habitually routine questions about how work was that day. When you take the time to continually get to know your spouse, you will grow closer to your spouse in greater fellowship.

Steps to Fellowship

Prayer

At the end of the Last Supper, Jesus took time to pray for the disciples (John 17:1-26). He understood that mere fellowship was not enough to spur the disciples to the calling God had laid before them. It took the intervention of God in the supernatural through prayer to prepare them for their calling. True fellowship requires prayer. The act of prayer is not just words, but is the solicitation of God into the relationship. It brings forth the power, the strength, and the gifts that are embedded deep within each of us. Praying with and for your spouse enables the supernatural to happen in your marriage. It brings God into the relationship.

Empathy

Even in the perfect fellowship between Jesus and God, Jesus still needed to pray. His prayers revealed His heart. They revealed His anguish. It demonstrated a complete openness with the Father. When Jesus expressed His anguish that was contrary to the will of God, God did not respond in wrath or anger. God responded with an angel to strengthen Him.

Jesus went out as usual to the Mount of Olives, and his disciples followed him. On reaching the place, he said to them, "Pray that you will not fall into temptation." He withdrew about a stone's throw beyond them, knelt down and prayed, "Father, if you are willing, take this cup from me; yet not my will, but yours be done." An angel from heaven appeared to him and strengthened him. And being in anguish, he prayed more earnestly, and his sweat was like drops of blood falling to the ground.

- Luke 22:39-44

Encouragement

When we encourage others, we draw closer in unity. This is a simple principle in all relationships. We want to be with those that affirm and esteem us. It is important to take time to let your spouse know what you appreciate about them and to encourage them daily.

Therefore, if you have any encouragement from being united with Christ, if any comfort from his love, if any common sharing in the Spirit, if any tenderness and compassion, then make my joy complete by being like-minded, having the same love, being one in spirit and of one mind.

- Philippians 2:1-2

And let us consider how we may spur one another on toward love and good deeds, not giving up meeting together, as some are in the habit of doing, but encouraging on another – and all the more as you see the Day approaching.

- Hebrews 10:24-25

Encouragement is also shown when we communicate appreciation for our spouse and the positive attributes they bring into the relationship. When we feel appreciated, we begin to take down walls of defensiveness that hinder fellowship.

Summary

Fellowship is about being one with your spouse. It involves a daily decision to not let anything separate that oneness and come between you. It is an intimate knowledge that occurs when you come together in unity and share your life with your spouse. Fellowship builds trust, enhances communication and allows a couple to truly experience each other in an intimate way.

God designed us for this type of fellowship and to experience it in our marriage, as well as in our relationship with him. It reflects the characteristics of God himself in the Trinity.

Bridge of Fellowship: Study Questions

What is Fellowship

Why do you think that God wanted man to reflect the image of the Trinity?

What attributes of the Trinity do you feel your marriage best reflects?

What are some things that originally attracted you to your spouse?

In what ways do we demonstrate our oneness in our marriage?

What are some ways that you get to know your spouse over time?

What are some ways that you and your spouse want to have an impact?

Why Fellowship is Important

Why do you think God chose marriage as the relationship that best reflects the Trinity?

How are you and your spouse working together to accomplish the work that God has set before you?

What are some ways that you could celebrate during a time of fellowship?

What are some traditions or ways that can help maintain and strengthen the fellowship you share with your spouse?

What Hinders Fellowship

What are some gods or idols you could put before God?

What are some gods or idols you could put before your spouse?

What are some ways that you could misuse your spouse's name?

In what way is selfishness demonstrated in marriage?

What are some ways you can avoid or prevent selfishness?

How do you handle difficult times and challenges in your marriage and do you have objective and qualified people to mentor you during these times?

What Promotes Fellowship

What do you think "living in the light" looks like in marriage?

In what ways do we establish a regular "Couple Sabbath" to devote time to each other in fellowship with minimal distractions?

What are some additional ways we could devote that time together?

Why is it important to allow your spouse to focus enough time on their responsibilities?

In what ways do we make it easy and/or difficult for our spouse to repent and forgive in our marriage?

How Fellowship is Demonstrated by God

What are some things that your spouse does or could do that would make you feel pursued?

What are some ways that fear can enter into a marriage relationship?

What are some other ways you can remind each other of your marriage covenant?

In what ways has God shown his protection in your life?

How Fellowship is Demonstrated in Marriage

What are some of the fun ways that we demonstrate our fellowship with one another?

What obligations do we have that interfere with the time we could spend together?

What are some new hobbies that we could enjoy together?

How healthy is your sex life? What are ways it could improve?

How healthy is the communication with your spouse?

Steps to Fellowship

How is your prayer life individually and as a couple?

What are some things that would help you make prayer a more regular part of the fellowship with your spouse?

What are some ways that we could "send an angel" to each other when we express our anguish?

What are some of the things you appreciate most about your spouse?

What skills, passions, ideas and attributes do each of you individually bring into our marriage that makes your marriage stronger than you as individuals?

Chapter 7: The **Bridge of Purpose**

If marriage is a journey, think of purpose as your compass. Purpose will help guide you through the challenges that you encounter and also can lead you towards your goals that will bring great fulfillment and joy in your marriage. Yet, it begs a common question.

What is my purpose? This is a question that has been asked throughout human history and one that everyone will ask themselves at some point in their life. We want to know why we are here and what we are called to do. Why is this so important? It is important because we want meaning in life. It is a common internal desire that God put in all of us. It draws us to him. Why? Because he is the only one that can answer it.

What is Purpose

Deliberate Motivation

Ephesians 1:11 says that "*In him we were also chosen, having been predestined according to the plan of him who works out everything in conformity with the purpose of his will.*"

The Greek word for purpose in this verse is *Boule*, which also carries a meaning of counsel, decision, motive and plan. This word comes from the root word *Boulomai*, which means to will deliberately, have a purpose and to be minded.

God is motivated by His purpose and is deliberate in His actions. When we have a deliberate motivation, it allows us to have conviction. It better equips us to make tough choices. When you are evaluating your purpose, it is important to understand what motivates you as a couple. What are you passionate about?

Godly Counsel

The second aspect of purpose is Godly counsel. Proverbs 19:21 says, *"Many are the plans in a man's heart, but it is the Lord's purpose that prevails."* Another translation of Proverbs 19:21, says that the counsel of the Lord will stand.

The Hebrew word for purpose and counsel in this verse is *'etsah*, which means counsel, advice or purpose. The concept of God's purpose providing advice and counsel to us is seen throughout scripture. Purpose provides us with the direction and guidance necessary to make wise decisions. The Hebrew word for stand or prevail in this passage is *quwm*, which means to rise up, be fixed, established, persist and fulfilled. In other words, God's counsel will create stability in your life. If that is the result of God's advice, why wouldn't we seek it?

Our purpose will also counsel and advise us as it influences our actions and decisions. It becomes a compass in our lives which guides us on our marriage journey.

Our Reflection

The final aspect of purpose is that it is our reflection. Romans 8:28 says, *"And we know that God causes all things to work together for good to those who love God, to those who are called according to his purpose."*

The Greek word for purpose in this verse is *Prothesis*, which means the setting forth of something and placing it in view. The root of this word is *Protithemai*, which means to set forth and expose something to public view and to set before or propose to one's self.

In Mark 2:26, Prothesis is also used in reference to shewbread, which were twelve loaves of consecrated bread in the Temple that were laid on the Table of the Presence (Exodus 25:23-30 and Leviticus 24:5-9). Shewbread literally means "bread of the face" as it was bread that was laid out before the face or presence of God.

When we think of purpose as being exposed to public view, we begin to see it as a reflection of who we are. It begins to define us individually and as a couple. And, when we are called according to His purpose, then we are essentially called according to a reflection of who God is and our calling is a reflection of God.

Ask yourself: (1) What motivates you; (2) What promptings of God have you experienced; and (3) What would you like your life and your marriage to reflect?

Why Purpose is Important

It is so crucial for a couple to develop and understand their collective purpose. Purpose is important because it: Reveals God's Will, Provides Direction, Gives us Strength and Creates Unity.

Reveals God's Will

Many people often ask, "What is God's will?" They want to know God's desire for them. In order to understand the mystery of God's will, we have to look to His purpose.

In Luke 22:42 Jesus says, *"Father, if you are willing, remove this cup from me; yet not my will, but yours be done."* The Greek word for will in this verse is *Thelema* which means what one wishes or has determined shall be done. It reflects as aspect of God that will not change when it is connected to his purpose. This includes what God wishes to be done by us and the purpose of God to bless mankind through Christ.

In Luke 22:42, Christ was able to distinguish between His will (desire) and God's will (desire) in that moment of agony, because He knew God's ultimate purpose. It gave Him clarity in the midst of what was becoming a chaotic and agonizing environment; allowing Him to make a very difficult decision.

<u>Direction</u>

The second aspect of the importance of purpose is that it provides direction. When we know our purpose, it allows us to venture into new callings in life with confidence. It guides us in unchartered territory and lets us know our next steps.

In Luke 4:42-43, we see Christ being accepted with praise by the local people of Capernaum, but He recognized the need to move on to other cities because He was sent for that purpose. In this passage it says, *"When the day came, Jesus left and went to a secluded place; and the crowds were searching for him, and came to him and tried to keep him from going away from them. But he said to them, "I must preach the kingdom of God to the other cities also, for I was sent for this purpose."*

How easy would it have been for Jesus to stay in that one place and enjoy the praise of men? It was comfortable, particularly after having just been run out of Nazareth and nearly thrown off a cliff (Luke 4:16-30). However, his understanding of his purpose gave him direction and the ability to see through the emotions. Without direction, we can get stuck in one place and never move forward in the calling that God has on our life and in our marriage. We get caught in a trap where we are comfortable and reluctant to change and ultimately find ourselves in a rut.

<u>Gives Us Strength</u>

Another important aspect of purpose is that it gives us strength. In John 12:27 we read about Jesus foretelling his death. We begin to see him start the process of agonizing internally about his death which later comes to a climax in the Garden of Gethsemane when he said, *"Now my soul has become troubled; and what shall I say, "Father, save me from this hour?" But for this purpose I came to this hour."* Christ knew his purpose and it gave him the strength to persevere during these most difficult times.

<u>Unity</u>

Finally, purpose is important because it builds unity. It brings people together in fellowship and creates an atmosphere of joy. Philippians 2:1-2 says, *"If you have any encouragement from being united with Christ, if any comfort from his love, if any fellowship with the Spirit, if any tenderness and compassion, then make my joy complete by being like-minded, having the same love, being one in spirit and purpose."*

The Greek word for purpose in this verse is *Phroneo*, which is actually a verb (something you actively do together) and describes having understanding and wisdom through being of the same mind harmoniously. Couples that work together to determine their common purpose will grow closer and experience each other in a unique and intimate way. It is that unity that will propel your marriage to greater strength. If you want to have a strong marriage, then you must have a clear purpose.

What Hinders Purpose

<u>Our Plans</u>

Many are the plans in a person's heart, but it is the Lord's purpose that prevails.

- *Proverbs 19:21*

But I said, "I have labored in vain; I have spent my strength for nothing at all. Yet what is due me is in the Lord's hand, and my reward is with my God.

- *Isaiah 49:4*

In reading these verses, one could easily misinterpret that their efforts and plans are useless and decide to not make any plans. Plans are however an important step in carry out our desires. The challenge becomes when we get ahead of God in our plans and do not seek his counsel. If we fail to seek God's counsel and are not moving in the direction of his purpose, only then do our plans become useless. However, it is important that we don't fail to do anything as we wait for God's counsel. God expects us to take responsibility in making our plans, but just be mindful to not make your plans without seeking the counsel of God.

Pride

The Pharisees and interpreters of the Law did not accept God's purpose for them because they were too proud to accept that they needed to repent of their sins and be baptized by John the Baptist.

> *But the Pharisees and the experts in the law rejected God's purpose for themselves, because they had not been baptized by John.*
>
> *- Luke 7:30*

Their focus on their own desires and beliefs prevented them from recognizing the counsel and purpose of God.

Too often, we can become too caught up in what we want out of life and end up rejecting or not seeking God's counsel with a pure and willing heart. God wants to reveal his purpose for us, but he needs us to approach him with a willing attitude to accept that purpose regardless of our own desires. The unfortunate thing for the Pharisees is that they ended up rejecting the very Messiah they were looking for.

Human Nature

One of the challenges we all face as humans is fighting against ourselves. We all suffer from our own sinful nature and wage an internal battle between God's counsel and our own desires (Acts 5:37-39 and Romans 7:14-25). This often creates an additional challenge for couples to understand their purpose since they not only have to discern their individual ideas, but also the ideas of their spouse. This can also be further complicated by each person's insecurities and feelings of inadequacy. Often times, God calls us into these difficult areas as a way of revealing his power and grace.

Our Company

The company you keep will often influence your steps. People love to give their advice and God often competes with our closest friends. He also often speaks to us through others. The point is to be careful when you take the advice of others and to pray together as to whether or not this counsel is from God.

Blessed is the one who does not walk in step with the wicked or stand in the way that sinners take or sit in the company of mockers, but whose delight is in the law of the Lord, and who meditates on his law day and night. That person is like a tree planted by streams of water which yields its fruit in season and whose leaf does not wither – what they do prospers.

- *Psalm 1:1-3*

Fear

In Exodus 14:10-14, the Israelites were scared of what the Egyptians might do to them if they were caught when they fled Egypt. Their fear could have prevented them from finding freedom and following the direction of God. Fear comes when we don't trust God's provision. Before we can move into the purpose God has for us, we have to trust him. We have to trust him with our finances, time, safety and relationships.

What Promotes Purpose

Understanding

The purposes of a person's heart are deep waters, but one who has insight draws them out.

- *Proverbs 20:5*

The word for purpose in this verse is *'etsah*, which we covered above and means purpose, counsel and advice. Our purpose is already deep within each one of us. The challenge is finding how to bring it to the surface. If we take the time to grow in our spiritual understanding or wisdom, we will begin to bring forth our purpose. When we spend time studying God's word and praying, we will increase our ability to discern and respond to the promptings of God. It is at this point that our internal purpose begins to emerge and become active in our lives.

Good Counsel

Not only is good counsel important to obtain, but it is also important to seek counsel from more than one person.

> *Plans fail for lack of counsel, but with many advisors they succeed.*
>
> *- Proverbs 15:22*

> *Plans are established by seeking advice; so if you wage war, obtain guidance.*
>
> *- Proverbs 20:18*

When we pray and obtain guidance from several people we trust, we will often begin to see a common thread emerge that will direct our steps. The final and most important counsel needs to be the counsel obtained from God. Remember that good counsel will never contradict or compromise scripture.

God's Word

God's word is living and active (Isaiah 55:10-11). When we take the time to meditate on God's words, we will begin to feel the prompting of the Holy Spirit as God directs our steps. Our purpose is often revealed in those quiet moments when we are praying and meditating on God's word. Don't neglect the power of these moments in your life as God may be reaching out to you.

Worship

We demonstrate our love of God through worship. Romans 8:28 says that "*all things work together for the good of those who love him, who have been called according to his purpose.*" We worship God through our actions, our songs of praise, and our prayers, among other ways. When we demonstrate our love and draw close to God, he will be able to work in our lives in unique ways. The Greek word for "called" in this verse is *kletos*, which carries a meaning of being divinely invited (such as to a banquet). When we show our love to God, he invites us alongside his purpose. It is up to us to accept the invitation.

How Purpose is Demonstrated by God

Consistent

God's purpose is eternal. It has no beginning and no end. He is deliberate in his purpose, and as noted in Hebrews 6:17, his purpose is unchanging. This means that it is not compromised or minimized.

Because God wanted to make the unchanging nature of his purpose very clear to the heirs of what was promised, he confirmed it with an oath.

- *Hebrews 6:17*

Unwavering

When God determines his purpose, he does not stop until that purpose is accomplished (Jeremiah 23:20). This requires conviction and underscores the importance in being sure of your purpose. When you're not confident in your purpose, you will be tossed around like the waves in the sea (James 1:5-7).

Foreknown

In the original Greek in Acts 2:23, it says that the handing over of Jesus was a "defined (*horizon*) purpose (*boule*)". God does not redefine or hesitate in defining his purpose for himself or you. He does not wait to see how things work out. Of course, God is omniscient and we are not. However, we can benefit from this in that he already has a purpose for us that we can seek. Ephesians 2:10 says that God has good works which he prepared in advance for us to do.

<u>Planned</u>

Not only does God foreknow his purpose, but he has a defined plan to accomplish that purpose (Psalm 33:11 and Ephesians 1:11). While it is important to know your purpose, it is also important to have a God inspired plan in place for how you will live out that purpose. This plan should reflect the unique talents, skills and desires that God has given to you.

How Purpose is Demonstrated in Marriage

<u>Pray for Each Other</u>

God works in our lives through the prayers that we offer. Colossians 1:9 expresses the need to continually pray for each other so that we will know the will of God. Fulfilling our purpose often requires significant emotional and spiritual strength and the prayers of others to help us through challenging times are essential. Couples that pray for each other and with each other will find greater clarity and strength as they fulfill their purpose.

<u>Encourage Each Other</u>

One of the greatest things you can do as a husband or wife is to encourage your spouse (Colossians 2:2). God modeled the need for encouragement by sending the Holy Spirit to serve as an encourager for each of us (2 Corinthians 1:3-4). We receive passion, strength and hope through the encouraging words and actions of our spouse. One of the key principles in offering comfort to others is to first allow God to comfort us. Once we experience his comfort, we will be empowered to offer that same comfort to our spouse.

<u>Commit Your Plans to God</u>

Once you have a plan to accomplish your purpose, it is important to commit it to God.

Commit your work to the Lord, and your plans will be established....A man's mind plans his way, but the Lord directs his steps.

- *Proverbs 16:3, 9*

God wants to be involved in our plans so that he can direct our steps, so that we will be successful. The Hebrew word for "commit" in Proverbs 16:3 is *galal*, which means to "roll together" and the word for "succeed" is *kuwn*, which means to be "stable or firmly established." These verses reveal that if we work with God to understand our purpose, then our purpose will be aligned with God's purpose. As we previously discussed, God's purpose is unwavering and will be firmly established. When he directs our steps, we can move forward in confidence that we will succeed in accomplishing our purpose. When you work together with your spouse as you commit your plans and purpose to God, you're marriage will also become even more firmly established.

Steps to Purpose

Be Still and Listen
When we take time to be still and quiet our spirit, we allow ourselves to hear God (Psalm 37:7 and Psalm 46:10). Too often, couples get so busy that they forget to take time to just rest and listen. It is during these moments of quiet meditation that God is able to fill our minds with his vision for our lives.

When reading the story in John 21:3-6, one can imagine the quietness on that boat with the disciples. After a night of not catching any fish, there was probably not much conversation. However, they were able to hear Jesus call out to them and take his advice. It is often in those times of discouragement that we will hear God if we have the willingness to listen. It is also not uncommon that in those times he asks us to step out in faith so that we will recognize him.

Cry Out

There are times that we just need to get on our knees and cry out to God for direction. In Psalm 57:2, David said that he cries out to God who fulfills his purpose for him. We need to have a passionate desire to know our purpose and a willingness to do whatever it takes to pursue it.

Seek Righteousness

When we seek righteousness, we will be drawn closer to God and will begin to hear God more clearly (2 Timothy 2:20-22). Sin separates us from God and makes it difficult for him to guide us in our purpose. This requires a confession of the sin in our lives, asking forgiveness and a willingness to turn away from that sin.

Be Diligent

Getting comfortable with your purpose often requires great diligence and patience. Proverbs 21:5 says *"The plans of the diligent lead surely to abundance, but ever one who is hasty comes only to want."* It is commonly said that those that are successful fail more often than they succeed. You may not fully understand your purpose immediately. It may require a path of challenges that prepare you for what God has planned for you. Your diligence during this period of development will be crucial to your success.

Summary

Purpose can be summed up as a reflection of the counsel of God in your life as he directs your steps towards his divine calling for you individually and as a couple to accomplish his will. When you determine your purpose individually and as a couple, and begin to work in concert with God, you will be drawn closer to him and closer together as a couple.

There are many things that prevent us from determining or accepting our purpose whether it is our plans, pride, fear or other influences in our life.

However, when we are willing to humble ourselves before God and meditate on his word and counsel, we will begin to understand our purpose.

God made each one of us in a unique way (Psalm 139: 13-16) to work with him to accomplish his purpose of bringing humanity into a relationship with him for eternity.

Bridge of Purpose: Study Questions

What is Purpose

What is God's motivation?

What motivates you individually and as a couple?

How would recognizing God's purpose as being his counsel and advice impact your decisions?

As a couple, how do you seek God's advice and counsel in making your decisions?

If you looked back at your decisions over the past year, what would it reveal as the guiding advice and counsel of your purpose?

What would others say your purpose is based on what your life reflects?

What are some things that you would like your life to reflect?

Why Purpose is Important

Do you have a difficult time understanding God's will?

How do you try to determine God's will?

What are some areas in your life where you are comfortable and reluctant to change?

Do you tend to see your next steps with clarity or confusion? Why?

What has gotten you through some of the greatest challenges in your life?

How often do you and your spouse talk about your common purpose?

What are some areas that you and your spouse are not of the same mind? What impact does it have on your marriage?

What Hinders Purpose

Why do you think God wants to be involved as we develop our plans?

How do you currently make your plans and do you struggle knowing whether they fit within God's purpose?

What are some ways you can be prideful towards God?

What are some ways we can be prideful towards your spouse?

How would you rate your willingness to accept God's purpose regardless of His calling? Why?

What are some ways that you struggle with your own desires?

Why is it important to take the time to determine whether your plans are yours or God's?

Which relationships do you have that encourage you to grow in your relationship with God?

How do we decide whether the counsel from others is good or bad?

What are your greatest fears?

How might the fears you have today impact your willingness to hear and accept God's purpose for you?

What Promotes Purpose

What are some ways that you can begin to grow more in your spiritual journey with God?

What are some ways that you can begin to grow more in your spiritual journey with your spouse?

What are some ways we can seek counsel from God?

How would you rate the counsel you have received from others in the past? Who are the people whose counsel you value the most and what makes it valuable?

How would you rate your time spent meditating on God's word?

What are some ways you could meditate on God's word with your spouse?

How do you worship God? What are some other ways you could worship him?

At what times do you feel closest to God?

How Purpose is Demonstrated by God

What in your life will not be compromised?

Why do you think it is important to have an unchanging/consistent purpose in your life?

Why is it important to know that God will not waiver in His purpose?

How would you rate your confidence in your purpose? What would increase your confidence?

What are the benefits of knowing your purpose sooner than later?

How does God having a foreknown purpose for you impact your decisions?

Why is it important to have a plan to accomplish your purpose?

What are your talents, skills and desires?

In what ways are your talents, skills and desires complimentary to your spouse's talents, skills and desires?

How Purpose is Demonstrated in Marriage

Do you know what your spouse would like you to pray for? How often do you talk about it with your spouse?

What are 10 things you would like your spouse to pray for you?

In what ways do you feel most encouraged by God?

In what ways do you feel most encouraged by your spouse?

How often do you and your spouse talk about your goals?

How would you describe your purpose as a couple?

How would you rate how well you and your spouse "roll together" your plans and purpose with God? What are some ways you could improve?

Steps to Purpose

How good are we at taking time to be still and quiet?

Do you feel like you are able to hear God? What are some things you could do to allow yourselves to hear him more clearly?

What was a time you stepped out in faith and saw God at work?

What do you really want to accomplish for the Kingdom of God individually and as a couple?

How would you currently describe your spiritual walk and closeness with God?

What are some ways you could pursue righteousness and draw closer to God?

What are some passions you have where you have been discouraged in the past?

How well do you handle set-backs? What could help you handle them better?

Chapter 8: The Bridge of Celebration

The final bridge is about celebrating your marriage! There is no doubt that God loves a good celebration. Throughout scripture we find God's people engaging in festivals and celebrations as a means to express their relationship with God. We see Jesus participating in a wedding celebration and celebrating the Passover with his closest friends. Relationships should be celebrated. Celebrations bring new life into the challenges of our everyday circumstances and remind us to take time to enjoy our marriage. It also demonstrates that we care about our spouse. Finding creative ways to celebrate your relationship with your spouse will bring passion and excitement into your marriage.

What is Celebration

We think about celebrations in the following categories: Planned Event, Spontaneous Event, Purposeful Event and a Remembrance Event.

Planned Events

In Numbers 9:2, it says *"Have the Israelites celebrate the Passover at the appointed time."* Celebrations are often held at specific times, and most are annual events. Celebrations can also be spontaneous (discussed below); however, planned celebrations have a unique value. It sets aside a time that we can look forward to with anticipation. It builds excitement within a relationship and usually celebrates a certain event (birthday, anniversary, holiday, etc.).

Spontaneous Events

For Spontaneous Events, we look to Luke 15:22-24 about the prodigal son. It says, *"The father said to his servants, 'Quick! Bring the best robe and put it on him. Put a ring on his finger and sandals on his feet. Bring the fattened calf and kill it. Let's have a feast and celebrate. For this son of mine was dead and is alive again; he was lost and is found.' So they began to celebrate."*

Spontaneous celebrations can sometimes be the most memorable. These celebrations typically celebrate a specific person or action by the person. They communicate that you value them and are willing to change your schedule to focus on them. In this passage, the father decides to spontaneously celebrate his son coming home. It communicated to his son, that he was not rejected based on his past actions and demonstrated the genuineness of his father's forgiveness. Finding ways to spontaneously celebrate your spouse or your marriage can often add a needed spark in the midst of our daily routines.

Purposeful

Celebrations may also be purposeful. Numbers 9:14 says, "'An alien living among you who wants to celebrate the LORD's Passover must do so in accordance with its rules and regulations. You must have the same regulations for the alien and the native-born." The purpose of the celebration often influences the development of traditions. Traditions are not rules to constrain the celebration, but are activities to provide an expectation and anticipation for the celebration, as well as help us understand what is being celebrated. Couples that develop their own traditions create a unique experience for them to share intimately. It allows them to express themselves as a couple.

Remembrance

Finally, Celebrations may be a time of Remembrance. Exodus 12:14 talks about the Passover and says, "This is a day you are to commemorate; for the generations to come you shall celebrate it as a festival to the LORD - a lasting ordinance." Celebrations are often about remembering past events. This is done to establish an importance of an event in our lives, so we (and others) don't forget the past, and to appropriately honor others.

Why Celebration is Important

Celebrations are critical for a growing and healthy relationship. They have 4 main purposes: Protecting your Relationship, Highlights the Value of your Relationship, Brings Blessings to your Relationship, and it Demonstrates Love.

Protecting Your Relationship

Many people don't think about celebrations protecting your relationship. Isaiah 30:29 says, *"And you will sing as on the night you celebrate a holy festival; your hearts will rejoice as when people go up with flutes to the mountain of the Lord, to the Rock of Israel."* Celebrations help your heart rejoice. A heart that regularly rejoices is less likely to become hardened and lose faith. When you lose heart in your marriage, then you leave the defenses that were established to protect your marriage. A hardened heart loses the desire for the relationship. How many times have you heard married couples say, "We used to go out together all the time" or "I don't remember the last time we had a date night." Those are the statements that begin to emerge when you fail to protect your marriage.

Highlights the Value of Your Relationship

Looking again at the parable of the prodigal son, it'd clear that celebrations give you the opportunity to bring attention and focus on what you want to celebrate. It highlights the value of what is being celebrated. In his passage, the father wanted to celebrate his son. He did this not just so that his son would realize the importance his father saw in him, but to also let the son's brother know the value the father saw in him. A celebration can help communicate that more than just with words.

Brings Blessing to Your Relationship

The next reason celebrations are important is that they bring blessings to the relationship. Deuteronomy 16:15 says, *"For seven days celebrate the Feast to the Lord your God at the place the Lord will choose. For the Lord your God will bless you in all your harvest and in all the work of your hands, and your joy will be complete."*

God promised to bless the Israelites in their harvest. He gave this promise with respect to the Feast of Tabernacles, which was done after the crops of the land were harvested. The Israelites were to give a portion of their harvest as part of the festival to honor God's provision. When we give up part of ourselves (financially, time, etc.) to celebrate others, it demonstrates a level of appreciation and can bring blessings into the relationship.

Shows Love

Finally, celebrations demonstrate love. Just before Jesus and the disciples began the Passover Feast in John 13:1-3, Jesus got up and demonstrated the extent of his love by washing the disciples' feet. In the midst of the feast, Jesus took the opportunity to demonstrate love in an astounding way. Celebrations offer us the opportunity to show our love for others in many ways, whether it is a toast, planning the celebration, giving gifts or other acts of service and appreciation.

What Hinders Celebration

Fear

When we are scared, we often don't feel like celebrating. Fear can be a crippling force and prevent us from even the desire to leave our home, let alone celebrate (Job 31:34). However, God is there to take away our fear (Psalm 46:1-3). When we free ourselves from fear, it opens up our heart and desire for celebration.

Look, there on the mountains, the feet of one who brings good news, who proclaims peace! Celebrate your festivals, Judah, and fulfill your vows. No more will the wicked invade you; they will be completely destroyed.

- Nahum 1:15

Resentment

The response of the prodigal son's brother in Luke 15:29-31 revealed a sense of resentment, and even entitlement. He refers to himself as "slaving" for his father and was never "given" a goat so he could celebrate with his friends. He clearly reveals that he felt that he was not compensated enough. However, the father's response was astounding. He said that everything he had was always available to his son. In other words, he didn't have to ask for a goat to be given.

When we allow ourselves to become resentful, we will become unaware of the blessings and opportunities that are already before us. Resentment makes us look for reasons to express anger; instead of reasons to celebrate.

Disobedience

Disobedience tends to remove a desire to celebrate. This can happen from feelings of guilt or the results of our actions that have dire consequences.

If the Egyptian people do not go up and take part, they will have no rain. The Lord will bring on them the plague he inflicts on the nations that do not go up to celebrate the Festival of the Tabernacles.

- Zechariah 14:18

Celebration either glorifies God or it doesn't. As noted in 1 Corinthians 10:21-22, we need to be careful that our celebrations are honoring to God and our spouse.

Unprepared

In 2 Chronicles 30:3, there is an interesting story about priests that were not prepared for the Passover celebration at the appointed time because they were not expecting to celebrate. Under the rule of the prior king, Hezekiah's father, the people of Judah had not celebrated the Passover at the temple in accordance with what was written. It is much harder to be ready to celebrate when we do not expect to celebrate. Being ready to celebrate is about having a heart and an attitude that embraces celebration and looks for those opportunities.

It is easy spend more time complaining with a poor attitude than looking for reasons to celebrate.

What Promotes Celebration

Cheerful Heart

All the days of the oppressed are wretched, but the cheerful heart has a continual feast.

- *Proverbs 15:15*

This is a great verse. A cheerful heart has a continual feast. When we focus on having a positive attitude, we are able to celebrate more freely. We can often choose how we view the world. We can view it through a negative or positive lens. Some people just choose to be negative. Choose a positive attitude and be ready to celebrate.

Understanding

In Nehemiah 8, Ezra brought out the Book of the Law of Moses and it was read to the people. When the people heard the words, they understood it and it says in verse 12 that "*all the people went away to eat and drink, to send portions of food and to celebrate with great joy, because they now understood the words that had been made known to them.*"

When we lack understanding of a situation, it can cause confusion or stress. This can make it difficult to celebrate. Confusion and stress can easily creep into a marriage relationship when couples don't communicate regularly. Without communication, there inevitably will be a lack of understanding within the relationship. Take time to talk regularly with your spouse about their views, feelings, dreams, goals, etc.

<u>Requests</u>

In 2 Chronicles 30:5, we read that King Hezekiah sent an invitation throughout Israel calling people to the Passover celebration. He set an example of asking others to celebrate! Some couples might find it helpful to take turns on a regular basis making a suggestion for a reason to celebrate.

<u>Focus</u>

When you focus on the goodness of God and understand how he is working in your life, it softens your heart and creates a desire to celebrate (Psalm 145:7). Similarly, when you focus on the goodness of your spouse and take the time to appreciate their acts of kindness, it softens your heart and creates a desire to celebrate with them.

<u>Cleansing</u>

Before King Hezekiah was able to have the Passover celebration, he had the temple cleansed (2 Chronicles 29:15-17). When we cleanse ourselves spiritually through repentance and cleanse our marriage through forgiveness, we enable ourselves to celebrate. Feelings of guilt, remorse, or even not measuring up can create an atmosphere that doesn't celebrate. If you want more excitement in your marriage, consider areas where you need forgiveness, as well as areas that you can offer forgiveness.

How Celebration is Demonstrated by God

<u>Forgiveness</u>

The parable of the prodigal son in Luke 15 is a story about God's forgiveness. Jesus describes God's desire to forgive as a father running to his son. The father's forgiveness not only made the father ready to celebrate, but it also freed his son of guilt, so he was able to celebrate. When we receive God's forgiveness, he wants us to celebrate with him.

Provision

We couldn't talk about God's desire for celebration without considering the story of Jesus turning water into wine in John 2. The miracle of Jesus turning water to wine is an expression of his desire to provide for us in all aspects, including celebration. God wants us to celebrate and is willing to provide in miraculous ways.

Sacred Assemblies

As we read in Leviticus 23, certain celebrations have a spiritual significance. They are times to give reverence to God and to focus on our own spiritual health. God clearly saw an importance in these celebrations and established seven separate celebrations for Israel. Each celebration had a unique spiritual purpose.

Instruction

In the midst of the celebration of the Last Supper (Matthew 26:17-30 and John 13-17), Jesus used it as a time to give instruction and guide the disciples' understanding of the events that would soon take place. This Passover feast had a particular importance, as Christ was about to become the Passover lamb. Christ used this opportunity to reveal the new covenant that was occurring in their midst. Celebrations are not always times for just rejoicing, but can also serve as a means of communicating an important message with an impact.

How Celebration is Demonstrated in Marriage

Passion

David and all Israel were celebrating with all their might before the Lord, with castanets, harps, lyres, timbrels, sistrums and cymbals.

- *2 Samuel 6:5*

Just as David and the whole house of Israel celebrated with all their might, couples should make a point to celebrate with passion. Get your heart into it. It is far too easy to become stagnant in even our celebrations. We choose the same restaurants, the same gifts, cut corners, etc. For your anniversary this year, do something different, and do it with passion. Your spouse knows when your heart is not in it and you are just going through the motions. If you want a marriage that is exciting, then make sure that you are doing your part and demonstrating the passion that you want reciprocated.

Special Occasions

A spouse forgetting their anniversary is one of the great fears shared by many.

> *When I fed them, they were satisfied; when they were satisfied, they became proud; then they forgot me.*
>
> -   *Hosea 13:6*

Certain events carry such a great importance that forgetting them can leave scares for many years. However, forgetting them is not the only thing that can leave a scare. Not taking the event serious and showing little interest can also leave similar, if not even greater scares. Know what is important to your spouse and take great care in celebrating those events.

Gifts

In Esther 9:22 we read about the giving of gifts. A gift can communicate many things to your spouse. It can communicate your level of passion for them. How much time did you spend finding the right gift? How much did you sacrifice? Does it reveal that you took time to really think about the perfect gift? Does it reveal that you have been listening to their comments about particular interests? Does it show that you thought about them in a special way when there was not a special event? Remember, the cost of gifts rarely come close to meaning as much as the thought and passion behind the gift.

Children

Couples need to make a point of celebrating their children. In Genesis 21:8, Abraham held a great feast to celebrate the weaning of Isaac. Look for opportunities to celebrate. It may be their first time sleeping through the night, when they are potty-trained, their first day of school, a time when they showed a caring heart, when they showed good sportsmanship, or when they did well on an exam at school.

Celebrating your children builds their confidence and shows them that you value and care about them.

Steps to Celebration

Be Joyful

Make all efforts to approach your current situations with joy. Remember that God is our source of joy (Psalm 19:8). Seek the guidance and counsel of God to bring you joy the in the midst of your circumstances.

Atmosphere

Creating an atmosphere in your home that embraces celebration is critical in giving your family the since that celebrating is okay. This includes the emotional stability of the home, as well. It is important that your family does not fear celebrations as times of anxiety, anger or guilt.

Deceit is in the hearts of those who plot evil, but those who promote peace have joy.

- Proverbs 12:20

Better a dry crust with peace and quiet than a house full of feasting, with strife.

- Proverbs 17:1

Seek God's Guidance

During the wedding celebration when Jesus turned water into wine, his mother instructed the servers at the wedding to do whatever Jesus asked (John 2:5). Jesus asked them to do something that would be considered odd by any account. During times when things look grim, seek God's guidance and do whatever he asks regardless of how odd it may seem. That is when the greatest miracles and times of celebration occur.

Resolve Conflict

We are called to do everything on our part to resolve conflicts quickly (Romans 12:18 and Ephesians 4:26). When we allow unresolved conflict to continue, it begins to build up bitterness in our lives and hardens our hearts. Set aside your desire to win arguments and be the first to forgive.

Plan It

Don't try to make all celebrations spontaneous. Take the time to plan out some celebrations just as King Hezekiah did in 2 Chronicles 30. Make it a priority.

Summary

Throughout scripture we find God's people engaging in festivals and celebrations as a means expressing their relationship with God. We see Jesus participating in a wedding celebration and celebrating the Passover with his closest friends. Relationships should be celebrated. Celebrations bring new life into the challenges of everyday life and remind us to take time to enjoy our marriage. It also demonstrates that we care about our spouse. Finding creative ways to celebrate your relationship with your spouse will bring passion and excitement into your marriage.

Bridge of Celebration: Study Questions

What is Celebration

What celebrations do you have?

What is your favorite celebration and why?

What types of spontaneous celebrations have you done?

What makes celebrations most memorable for you?

What types of traditions do you have?

What are some other types of traditions you could establish?

What were the 5 most significant events in your life? Do you celebrate them?

Why Celebration is Important

What was your most memorable evening?

What do you currently do to protect your marriage?

What are some things you value but may not demonstrate how much you value them?

What is the hardest thing for you to give up?

What could you give up as part of a celebration of your marriage to demonstrate your level of appreciation?

What are some ways you would feel most loved by your spouse?

What Hinders Celebration

What do you fear the most and why?

Are there any things that you feel resentful about?

What are some ways to overcome a resentful attitude?

What are some ways we can be disobedient to the ways God wants us to treat our spouse?

What are some examples of dishonoring celebrations?

What are some ways that we could be prepared to celebrate more frequently?

What Promotes Celebration

What are some positive things currently going on in your life?

How often do you spend time talking intimately with your spouse without distractions?

What makes it difficult to communicate more regularly?

What are some ways you could ask each other to celebration more frequently?

What are the ways that your spouse feels the most loved?

What qualities do you appreciate most about your spouse?

Are there any things that you need to cleanse in your marriage?

How Celebration is Demonstrated by God

How do you celebrate with God?

What are some ways that God has provided for you in the past?

What are ways that you provide for your spouse?

What celebrations do you have with a spiritual significance?

What do you do differently for these celebrations to recognize the spiritual significance?

How do you typically communicate important messages?

How Celebration is Demonstrated in Marriage

What was your most memorable evening with your spouse and what made it so special?

What are some new ideas for celebration?

What are the most important events that you feel should be celebrated?

What was your favorite gift that you ever received? What made it so special?

What types of celebrations did you have as a child?

What are some ways you could celebrate your children?

Steps to Celebration

When do you feel most joyful?

What are some things you could do to make your home more joyful?

How would you describe the atmosphere of your home?

How would you describe the emotional stability of your relationship during the holidays or other special occasions?

How do you seek God's guidance?

When do you feel you connect most with God?

What circumstances are you currently going through that you would like God's guidance?

Do you have any unresolved conflict in your marriage?

What do you find the most difficult about letting go of past conflicts?

What are some celebrations you could start planning?

Appendix

Couch Time! Questions

Communication at an intimate level is essential for a healthy and growing relationship. While many couples appreciate the importance of learning "how" to communicate more effectively, they should also recognize the importance of "what" and "how often" they are communicating. Getting to know your spouse doesn't stop once you say, "I do." When you take the time to continually learn about your spouse's dreams, experiences, fears, anxieties, hopes, struggles, passions and goals, you will find that your relationship with your spouse will grow and strengthen.

Couch Time is about taking at least 15 uninterrupted minutes at least once a week to discuss a Couch Time question. These questions are inspired by The Seven Bridges and are designed to guide couples in their marriage journey. We believe that you will experience a greater level of intimacy with just a little Couch Time!

Helpful Hint: Be sure to ask further questions to really understand and appreciate your spouse's answers. The goal is to create a dialogue and not just state an answer. Find out why their answer is so important to them, what makes them feel a particular way and how it relates to your marriage and family.

Humility

1. In what ways can humility be demonstrated in a marriage?

2. What is your greatest weakness and why?

3. What strength of your spouse is most needed in your life?

4. Describe a time your spouse did something unselfishly for you that meant a lot. Why was it so special?

5. What is something you could do as a couple to make a personal sacrifice to benefit someone else?

6. Describe an area where you'd like to show greater appreciation for your spouse?

7. What would be the hardest thing for you to give up for others? Why would it be so hard?

Forgiveness

1. What has been the hardest thing to forgive in your life and why?

2. What is the greatest thing you have ever been forgiven of by a person?

3. Do you find it harder to forgive or receive forgiveness and why?

4. What is the hardest thing about forgiving others?

5. How do you know when you've forgiven someone?

6. What is one thing you'd like to ask forgiveness for from your spouse?

7. In what ways do you think forgiveness is beneficial?

8. Do you have any things you haven't forgiven? If not, why?

Healing

1. What has been the hardest thing for you to overcome and why?

2. What is your greatest fear and why?

3. What was your most painful experience and why?

4. What things does your spouse do that makes you feel most appreciated?

5. What are you currently most stressed about and why?

6. In what ways do you think you've grown during your marriage?

7. What was the nicest thing your spouse has done for you and what did mean to you?

8. What are two things you'd like to do differently in your marriage than you saw in your parent's marriage?

Patience

1. What has been the hardest thing to wait for since you've been married?

2. What would be most worth the wait?

3. What are you most thankful for in how your spouse has been patient with you?

4. What is currently one of your greatest challenges to overcome?

5. What are three areas where you'd most like to see yourself grow personally?

6. What was one thing you had to wait the longest for? What made the wait so difficult?

Fellowship

1. What are three new activities we could do together in our free time?

2. What are the pros and cons in your communication style (1) during fun times, (2) during times of stress, and (3) when you are tired?

3. Describe your favorite time working with your spouse to accomplish a task or goal. What made that time so special?

4. What activities do you most enjoy experiencing with your spouse and why?

5. What activities or obligations do we have that are not essential and may take away from time we could spend together?

6. What are some of your favorite family traditions and why?

7. What are three new family traditions could we start and why?

8. What is one thing you've never told your spouse?

Purpose

1. What are three family goals you would like to see accomplished within the next 10 years?

2. What unique skills does each of us bring to our marriages that complement each other?

3. What are you passionate about and why?

4. What are three types of service activities that we could do together to help others?

5. What would you do differently if you had complete financial independence? Why would you do those things?

6. What dreams did you have as a child? How have they evolved?

7. What are three changes you could make in how you spend your money? Why would you make those changes?

8. How could you better support your spouse in their desires and ambitions?

Celebration

1. What did you think about each other after your first date? How has that evolved over time?

2. What was your favorite family vacation as a child? What made it so special?

3. What was your favorite evening since we've been married? What made it so special?

4. What would be the most exciting anniversary celebration we could have?

5. What would be the three most exciting places for us to vacation and why?

6. What do you most appreciate about your spouse and why?

7. What was the time that you laughed the most together?